3 133   0477 9098

3-01

10 JC
629.22
CAR

D1075602

ILLUSTRATED ENCYCLOPEDIA

TRACTORS
A VISUAL HISTORY

ILLUSTRATED ENCYCLOPEDIA

TRACTORS
A VISUAL HISTORY

JOHN CARROLL

LORENZ BOOKS

ACKNOWLEDGEMENTS

The publishers would like to thank the following picture libraries and photographers for the use of their pictures in the book:

Agripicture: 26bl (Peter Dean); 77tl (Peter Dean); Alpha Stock: 15b, tl; 16tl, bl; 17bl; 28r; 80bl; John Bolt: 30bl; 31tr, ml, bl; 33bl; 35tr; 45tr, br; 47br; 50b; 56bl; 65br; 77mr; 84mr, bl; 88bl; 89tr, mr, br; 90tr, mr; 91br, bl; 94tl; 95tl, tr; John Carroll: 14 all; 16tr; 29bl; 60tr, bl; 62; 66tl; 79mr; 85mr, br, bl; 87ml; 88br; 92bl; 95bl; CDC: 24-5 (Orde Eliason); 46br (Orde Eliason); 57br (Judy Boyd); 58; 59tr (Orde Eliason), b (Orde Eliason); 88tr; Ian Clegg: 65mr; Impact: 29ml (Alain le Garsmeur), t (Alain le Garsmeur), mr (Alain le Garsmeur); 75ml (Erol Houssein); 78br (Tony Page); Imperial War Museum: 35b; 36tr, br; 37br; 55b; 72mr; 81tr; 86mr, ml; Massey Ferguson: 89bl; Andrew Morland: 1m; 2; 3m; 5m; 6; 7b; 10 all; 11 all; 12tr, r; 13br; 18bl; 19br, tl; 20br, tl; 21b, tl; 22tl, br; 23t, bl; 27br; 32all; 33mr; 34bl; 35ml, bl, tl; 35; 36tl, mr; 37ml, tl, mr, tr; 44bl; 46tl; 52bl; 53bl, tr; 54 bl, tr; 55t; 67tl; 81b; 82b, m; 83t, bl, br; 86tr, bl; 87bl, ml; 92tr, br; 93t, b; Public Record Office Image Library: 87tr; Ann Ronan Picture Library: 12bl; 13tl, t, r; 14tr; 17br; 74tr; Rural History Centre, University of Reading: 48m; Spectrum Colour Library: 38-39; 49t; 73tr; 74bl; 75mr; 89tr; Still Pictures: 64b; 77ml; 79br (Pierre Gleizes), bl (Jeff Greenberg); 91tl (Mark Edwards); Tony Stone Images: 8-9 (Peter Dean); 47t (Colin Raw); 50tl (Gary Moon); 68-9 (Mitch Kezar); 70b (Peter Dean); 71mr (Arnulf Husmo); 72tl (Bruce Forster) 1/4 pg; 73tl (Kevin Horan); 75br (Bruce Forster); 78bl (Wayne Eastep); 79mr (Jerry Gay); Gary Stuart: 26tl; 27t; 28tr, bl; 33tr; 34tr; 40r, bl; 41tl, tr, br; 42tl, br; 43t, bl, br; 44tr; 45bl; 48bl, ml, br; 49br; 50tr; 51br, t; 64 tr, m; 65tl; 66 br; 67br; 70mr; 71br, tl, tr; 72br, bl; 73br, bl, mr; 75tl; 76tr, mr, bl; 77tr, mr, b; 78mr, tr; 79tr; 82t; 84tr, br; 90bl; Superstock: 12tl; 18tr; 30tr; 56tr; 57tl; 70t; 74br; Tank Museum Collection: 19tr; 52tr; 61; 63br; tl; 79tr; 80tr, mr; 81ml, mr; 85t Jacket Photography provided by The Stock Market

t=top b=bottom l=left r=right
m=middle tr=top right tl=top left
ml=middle left mr=middle right
bl=bottom left br=bottom right
lm=left middle

This edition first published in 2000 by Lorenz Books

Lorenz Books is an imprint of
Anness Publishing Limited
Hermes House
88-89 Blackfriars Road
London SE1 8HA

Published in the USA by Lorenz Books
Anness Publishing Inc., 27 West 20th Street, New York, NY 10011;
(800) 354-9657

This edition distributed in Canada by Raincoast Books
8680 Cambie Street, Vancouver, British Columbia V6P 6M9

A CIP catalogue record for this book is available from the British Library

ISBN 0-7548-0471-2

Publisher: Joanna Lorenz
Senior Editor: Joanne Rippin
Designer: Michael Morey
Picture Researcher: John Bolt

Previously published as part of a larger compendium,
The World Encyclopedia of Tractors & Farm Machinery

Printed and bound in Hong Kong

1 3 5 7 9 10 8 6 4 2

CONTENTS

Introduction   6

The Mechanization of Farming   8

The Evolution of the Tractor   24

The Innovators   38

The Trend to Specialization   68

Index   96

INTRODUCTION

Tractors are an everyday sight and are taken for granted as an essential farming
tool. However, tractors were not always so ubiquitous and the complete
mechanization of farming has only been achieved recently. In some cases the
mechanization of farming did not take place until the years after World War II.
America and Great Britain were among the nations that pioneered the tractor
and subsequent developments, such as the combine harvester, but both were
trailed by other nations. This book takes a look at the history and development
of the tractor as we now know it, and examines a number of the important people
whose efforts speeded up the development of farming machinery.

■ OPPOSITE *A 1923 12hp Lanz.*
Through use of a simple and
reliable design Lanz became the
predominant tractor maker
in Germany.

■ LEFT *At the beginning of the*
1900s Case diversified into the
manufacture of gasoline tractors
after the success of its
threshing machines.

The Mechanization of Farming

The mechanization of agriculture is often considered to have begun with the 18th-century inventions of Jethro Tull's mechanical seed drill of 1701 and Andrew Meikle's threshing machine, patented in 1788, but these inventions built on far older technology. Carvings excavated at the Babylonian city of Ur show that wheeled carts were in use as early as 4000 BC. They are also known to have been used in India shortly afterwards. Knowledge of this invention spread so that by 2000 BC the use of wheels had reached Persia, and then Europe by about 1400 BC. Initially the wheels were fixed to an axle and the whole assembly rotated, but this was later refined so that just the wheels rotated. Many kinds of animals were used to pull carts, including oxen, water buffalo, donkeys, horses, camels, elephants and even slaves. Tracks, and then roads, suitable for use by primitive vehicles were built. The next development of equivalent importance was the mechanical means of propulsion.

THE AGE OF STEAM

Experimentation with steam power began as early as the first century AD, when Hero of Alexandria, a Greek mathematician and inventor, developed the aeolipile, a primitive form of steam engine. It consisted of a hollow sphere that was filled with water and heated so that the expulsion of a jet of steam through a nozzle produced thrust. This device was a major step towards self-propelled machines. In the 15th century Leonardo da Vinci worked on designs for mechanisms that would convert reciprocating movement into rotary movement, to enable a wheel to be driven. He also considered the workings of what is now known as a differential, by which two wheels on a common axle could describe curves of different radii at differing speeds.

In 1599 Simon Stevin (1548–1620) built a sail-rigged and tiller-steered cart and recorded some wind-powered journeys along flat Dutch beaches. At around the same time an Italian physicist, Giambattista della Porta (1535–1615) began experimentation with steam pressure. He constructed a steam pump that was capable of raising water and realized that there must be a way to harness this idea to

■ ABOVE *Once the technology of steam engines was proven it was developed rapidly for agricultural use. Buffalo-Pitts of New York made this 16hp machine in 1901.*

■ RIGHT *Early tractors, using engines other than steam for propulsion, adopted a steam engine configuration as shown by this 1903 10–22hp two-cylinder Ivel.*

■ ABOVE *Minneapolis Threshing Machine were among early manufacturers of steam traction engines and threshing machines dating back to 1874. This is a 45hp model of 1907.*

■ LEFT *This working machine is a Corn Maiden, a Ruston steam traction engine that was manufactured in Lincoln, England in 1918.*

provide a means of propulsion. One of della Porta's pupils, Solomon de Caus, was intent on trying out the idea of steam propulsion in France but was incarcerated in an asylum at the instigation of members of the French clergy who disapproved of such experimentation. Another Italian, Giovanni Branca, combined della Porta's and de Caus's ideas and built a steam turbine. Steam from the boiler escaped through a nozzle into the perforated rim of a wheel and so turned it. Branca coupled this through a gear to a grinding machine and published an account of his experiments in 1629. Meanwhile another Jesuit, Jean de Hautefeuille (1647–1724), was experimenting with an internal combustion engine of sorts that used small amounts of gunpowder as the fuel.

A piston and cylinder were first employed in connection with steam by a French physicist, Denis Papin (1647–1712). In 1690 he designed a machine that used water vapour to move the piston inside the cylinder. The water within the cylinder was heated externally; as it vaporized it moved the piston upwards, then as it cooled the vapour condensed and the piston moved downwards through gravity. By 1707 the device was working well enough to power an engine in a boat. Unfortunately the local boatmen who had watched Papin testing his machine saw it as a threat to their livelihood and destroyed both the engine and the craft.

The first commercially successful atmospheric steam engine is acknowledged to have been the machine patented in 1698.

■ LEFT *Horses were the primary source of power until widespread acceptance of the tractor. Many early adverts suggested that, unlike horses, tractors only "ate" when hungry.*

■ TOP RIGHT *The large machine such as this 1912 locomotive-style 18hp Avery would be superseded by smaller, more compact, machines in a decade.*

■ BOTTOM RIGHT *Nichols, Shepard and Co made this 20–70hp steam engine but later were one of the four companies that merged to form Oliver Farm Equipment in 1929.*

An English military engineer, Captain Thomas Savery (1650–1715), designed and built a pistonless mechanism for raising water, which became known as "The Miner's Friend".

Worthwhile experiments with steam power continued and led to the manufacture of workable engines. Amongst the early machines was the steam pump invented by Thomas Newcomen (1663–1729), that combined ideas from both Papin and Savery. Newcomen

■ BELOW *The mechanization of farming began with developments such as Jethro Tull's version of the plough (Figure 1) as well as rolling (Figure 7) and harrowing (Figure 6).*

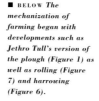

constructed a more efficient and less dangerous atmospheric steam engine and he formed a partnership with Savery, who possessed a general patent for such devices. The first practical engine was built in 1712. The pair refined the low-pressure atmospheric steam engine to the degree that most mines in Britain were using one by 1725. Across the Atlantic, the first low-pressure steam engine was installed in a copper mine in Belleville, New Jersey in 1753.

Meanwhile, Nicholas Cugnot (1725–1804), a French army engineer, built a steam-powered artillery carriage in 1769. This vehicle was the first machine designed especially for haulage and it could be said that this was when the era of mechanically propelled transport began. Cugnot's invention established Paris as the birthplace of the automobile in all its forms. His machine was a rudimentary three-wheeled vehicle, capable of speeds of up to 6.5kph/ 4mph. It was demonstrated on the streets of Paris, when it carried four people. The potential of Cugnot's invention was not perceived immediately and lack of support prevented its further development.

Technological advances specifically for agricultural purposes included Jethro Tull's seed drill and Andrew Meikle's invention of

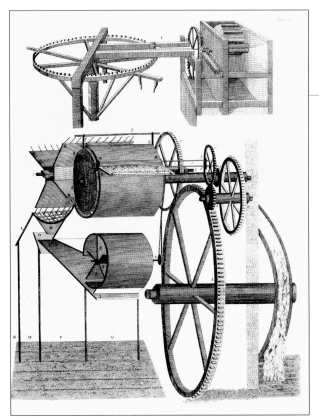

the mechanical thresher. Jethro Tull (1674–1741) devised a workable horse-drawn seed drill which dropped seed in rows. Andrew Meikle was a millwright from Dunbar in Scotland who, in the 1780s, developed a threshing machine for removing the husks from grain. Henceforward, after centuries in which farming techniques had changed little, the pace of development increased dramatically.

■ ABOVE RIGHT TOP *This illustration from 1756 shows the horse-drawn hoe-plough developed by Jethro Tull in the late 17th century.*

■ ABOVE RIGHT BOTTOM *Abbe Soumille's 18th-century seed drill which still relied on the power of human muscle.*

■ ABOVE *An 1811 engraving of Andrew Meikle's threshing machines. The top one is powered by a horse while the later one used a waterwheel.*

■ RIGHT *Threshers were further developed, as shown by this Oliver Red River Special of 1948 threshing in Illinois.*

STEAM POWER TO
GASOLINE ENGINES

■ BELOW *From 1876 Case manufactured in excess of 35,000 steam engines before shifting its entire production to gasoline tractors during the 1920s.*

In Britain in the 1780s and '90s, William Murdock (1754–1839) and Richard Trevithick (1771–1833) experimented with steam-powered vehicles using steam at above atmospheric pressure. A Welsh inventor, Oliver Evans (1755–1819), who had emigrated to America and lived in Maryland, produced an elementary steam wagon in 1772. In 1787 he was granted the right to manufacture steam wagons in the State of Maryland. His wagons never went into production but he did build a steam-powered amphibious dredging machine in 1804, which he engineered to be driven under its own power from its place of manufacture to the River Schuylkill, where it was launched for its voyage to Delaware. In 1788 a vehicle of a similar configuration, known as The Fourness, had been assembled in Britain.

In America in 1793 Eli Whitney patented the steam-powered cotton gin, which mechanized the cleaning of cotton fibre. This made cotton a commercial commodity in the eastern states, assisted by the growing transport network – including transcontinental railroads – around the United

■ ABOVE *Steam engines worked in pairs and pulled a large plough backwards and forwards across a field by means of the cable on the drum under the boiler.*

■ LEFT *The angled lugs arranged at intervals around the circumference of the driven wheels were intended to aid traction in wet and heavy soils.*

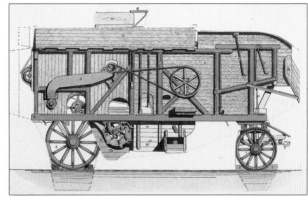

■ ABOVE LEFT *By the late 19th century, threshers were portable and powered by a steam engine. This later one has pneumatic tyres.*

■ ABOVE RIGHT *A portable threshing machine from around 1895. It had wooden-spoked wheels and was belt-driven by the steam engine that towed it.*

■ BELOW *Despite such mechanization, threshing was still a complex and labour intensive process as this vintage thresher shows.*

States. Thomas Blanchard, from Springfield, Massachusetts produced a steam carriage in 1825 and a year later, in New Hampshire, Samuel Morey patented a two-stroke gasoline and vapour engine – this was America's first internal combustion engine.

Early farm implements were drawn by horses but in order to make them more productive it was clear that there was a need for an independent mechanical source of power. The advent of road travel and the railway locomotive again focused attention on the possibilities of steam-powered machinery that was independent of both roads and rails. Gradually the technology began to diversify:

the steam traction engine became more refined and a practical proposition for farm use, while experiments proceeded with the gasoline-powered, internal combustion engine. American steam pioneers included Sylvester Roper of Roxbury, Massachusetts, John A. Reed from New York City, Frank Curtis from Massachusetts and the Canadian Henry Seth Taylor. Generally speaking at this time, the steam traction engine was reserved for providing power for driving equipment such as threshing machines.

New inventions took place throughout the 19th century, and these transformed farming practice. Cyrus McCormick's reaper of 1831

was to revolutionize grain-harvesting. In 1837, John Deere developed a self-scouring steel plough especially suited to heavy prairie soils: farmers no longer had to stop constantly to clean their ploughs. In 1842, in Rochester, Wisconsin, Jerome Case perfected a machine that was both a thresher and a fanning mill. In 1859 oil was discovered in Pennsylvania and kerosene and gasoline were distilled from it. Kerosene was immediately a popular choice as a fuel oil because it was cheap.

In the closing years of the 19th century, vehicles powered by internal combustion engines started to make an appearance and names like Nikolaus Otto, Karl Benz, Gottlieb

■ ABOVE RIGHT *Charles W. Hart and Charles H. Parr began pioneering work on gasoline tractors in the late 1800s in Wisconsin. They began the manufacture of machines such as this one in Iowa in 1900.*

■ BELOW *An English Fowler steam ploughing engine, no 15516, built in 1920 in Leeds, Yorkshire.*

Daimler, Wilhelm Maybach, Albert De Dion, Clement Panhard and Armand Peugeot became prominent in Europe as a result of their efforts. Of these, it is the first who made the greatest mark as he patented the four-stroke gas-powered engine. When Otto's patents expired in 1890 the age of the internal combustion engine dawned. It was but a short step to the development of a practical agricultural tractor.

Companies specializing in agricultural equipment were active around the globe. In 1870 Braud was founded in France to manufacture threshing machines. In 1884 Giovanni Landini started a new company in Italy to manufacture agricultural implements, that went on to become a major tractor maker. In the United States in 1895 the New Holland Machine Company was founded in Pennsylvania and specialized in agricultural equipment. The J. I. Case Threshing Company had been formed in 1863 to build steam tractors. Its first experimental tractor appeared in 1892, powered by a balanced gas engine devised by an engineer called William Paterson. The machine was not as successful as its designers had hoped, however, and it never went into commercial production. Case continued to build large steam engines. John Charter built gas engines in Stirling, Illinois

■ BELOW *An illustration of an earlier Fowler ploughing engine from c1862. The flywheel for the steam engine is located on the side of the boiler and the governor towards the rear.*

and manufactured a tractor by fitting one of his engines to the chassis and wheels of a steam traction engine. The resultant hybrid machine was put to work on a wheat farm in South Dakota in 1889. It was a success and Charter is known to have built several more machines to a similar specification.

By 1892 a number of other fledgling manufacturers were starting to produce tractors powered by internal combustion engines. In Iowa, John Froëlich built a machine powered by a Van Duzen single-cylinder engine, and formed the Waterloo Gasoline Traction Engine Company. The company later dropped the word "Traction" from its name and manufactured

■ ABOVE RIGHT *Before ploughing engines worked in pairs the concept of drawing the plough backwards and forwards relied on an anchor and pulley wheel.*

■ BELOW LEFT *A Fowler ploughing engine demonstrating drawing a five furrow anti-balance plough across the field.*

■ BELOW RIGHT *A mid-19th century illustration of a Garret and Sons steam engine ploughing across a field in England.*

only stationary engines until it introduced another tractor in 1916, the Waterloo Boy, the first successful gasoline tractor.

The Huber Company of Marion, Ohio had some early success: it purchased the Van Duzen Engine Company and built 30 tractors. Two other companies, Deering and McCormick, were building self-propelled mowers at this time; they were later to unite to become International Harvester. It was clear that the speed of mechanization of American farming was increasing. The name "tractor" was coined in 1906 by Hart-Parr, which had made its first gasoline tractor in Charles City, Iowa in 1902, and merged with Oliver in 1929.

THE BEGINNINGS OF MASS PRODUCTION

The contrasting economic conditions facing farming on either side of the Atlantic prior to World War I meant that America was where the majority of tractor production took place. Because of the differing sizes of farms on the two continents, designs that were specific to American prairie cultivation began to emerge and machines designed for drawbar towing of implements, especially ploughs, were experimented with.

The International Harvester Corporation was formed in 1902 through the merger of McCormick and Deering. Along with other companies, such as Avery, Russell, Buffalo-Pitts and Case, they built experimental machines at the beginning of the 20th century. Case built one in 1911 and by 1913 the company was offering a viable gasoline-powered tractor. Another early tractor was manufactured by two engineers, Charles Hart

and Charles Parr. Although this first model was heavy and ungainly, they quickly went on to produce more practical machines, including the 12-27 Oil King. By 1905 the company was running the first factory in the United States dedicated solely to the manufacture of tractors. Many early tractors were massive machines styled after steam engines, because their

■ ABOVE *The increasing mechanization in farming inevitably led to mass production as demand for machines grew. This is a 1930 Case corn planter.*

■ LEFT *International Harvester was among the first makers of gasoline tractors and made more than 600 of these Type A Mogul tractors between 1907 and 1911. This is a 1908 model.*

makers assumed that the new gasoline-powered machines would simply replace steam engines as a source of power and perhaps did not envisage the much wider role that tractors would come to play in farming. The trend to smaller tractors started in the second decade of the 20th century. Among the pioneers who made small tractors were the Bull Tractor Company with a three-wheeled machine, Farmer Boy, Steel King, Happy Farmer, Allis-Chalmers and Case. The latter manufactured the 10-20 in 1915.

As early as 1912, the Heer Engine Company of Portsmouth, Ohio produced a four-wheel-drive tractor. The Wallis Tractor Company produced a frameless model known as the Cub in 1913 while, six years earlier, the Ford Motor Company had built the prototype of what was intended to become the world's first mass-produced agricultural machine. The company did not actually start mass production of its first tractor, the Fordson Model F, until 1917. The frameless design, light weight and automobile-style method of production meant that the Ford Motor Company was soon among the industry leaders in tractor manufacture.

Many early tractors were built with two-cylinder engines as their source of power but

■ ABOVE LEFT Huber Manufacturing of Marion, Ohio started by manufacturing steam engines but moved into gasoline tractor manufacture in 1911. By 1925 its Super Four model was rated at 18–36hp.

■ ABOVE RIGHT Henry Ford designed the Fordson tractor in an attempt to do for farmers what the mass-produced Model T car had done for motorists in general.

■ RIGHT Case continued to produce threshing machines alongside tractors after its first prototype gasoline model was completed in 1892.

even this allowed for a variety of configurations, including horizontally opposed cylinders, vertical and horizontal twins and the design of crankshafts, which varied as engineers sought to make engines as powerful and reliable as possible. John Deere's two-cylinder machines earned their "Johnny Popper" nickname from

■ LEFT *Henry Ford was unable to call his tractors Fords because the name was coined by a rival manufacturer. His 1917 Fordson was, however, far more successful than its rival.*

the distinctive exhaust note created by a crankshaft on which the con rods were offset by 180 degrees. The theory behind the offset crankshaft was that it would eliminate much of the engine's vibration. J. I. Case favoured the horizontally opposed twin in an attempt to minimize vibrations.

The popularity of tractors soared and, while a handful of only six tractor makers were recorded in the United States in 1905, there were in excess of 160 operating by 1920. Many of these companies were not realistic long-term propositions and others were bankrupted by the Wall Street Crash, while a number of companies all but disappeared in mergers.

In Britain, Hornsby of Lincoln was building tractors by the 1890s. Its first model, the Hornsby-Akroyd Patent Safety Oil Traction Engine, was completed in 1896. It weighed 8.5 tons and was powered by an oil-burning Stuart and Binney engine that was noted for its reliability. The engine was started by means of a blowlamp that created a hot spot in the cylinder head and so allowed the single-cylinder engine to fire up without the need for an electric starting mechanism. Hornsby used a 20hp engine with a horizontal cylinder for its tractor and constructed four of these machines.

One of them was exhibited at the Royal Show in 1897 and was awarded the Silver Medal of the Royal Agricultural Society of England. In September of that year a landowner called Mr Locke-King bought one of the tractors: this was the first recorded sale of a tractor in Britain. The Hornsby Company supplied various machines to the British War Office with a view to military contracts, and experimented extensively with crawler tracks. The patents that it took out for these tracks were later sold to the Holt concern in the United States.

Petter's of Yeovil and Albone and Saunderson of Bedford both built tractor-type machines. Dan Albone was a bicycle manufacturer with

■ BELOW *The Hart-Parr 28–50 was a four-cylinder tractor of a basic design that endured in two- and four-cylinder types until Hart-Parr merged into the Oliver Farm Equipment company.*

■ ABOVE *In 1917 the 8–16 Junior was introduced by International Harvester in response to the demand for smaller and cheaper tractors, and asserted IH's position as a tractor maker.*

no experience of the steam propulsion industry, so he approached the idea of the tractor from a different viewpoint. He combined ideas from the automobile industry with those of agriculture and built a tractor named after the River Ivel.

Albone's machine was a compact three-wheeled design, which was practical and suited to a variety of farm tasks. It was a success and went into production; some machines were exported and the company would no doubt have become a major force in the industry had

it not been for Albone's death in 1906. The company ceased production in 1916.

Herbert Saunderson was a blacksmith who went to Canada where he became involved with farm machinery and the Massey-Harris Company. He returned to Britain as that company's agent and imported its products. Later he branched out into tractor manufacture on his own account. Initially Saunderson built a three-wheeled machine because Albone's Ivel was attracting considerable attention at the time. Later, in 1908, a four-wheeled machine was constructed and the company grew to be the largest manufacturer and exporter of tractors outside the United States. A later model was the Saunderson Universal Model G. When World War I started, Saunderson was the only company in Britain large enough to meet the increasing demand for tractors. In the mid-1920s Saunderson sold his business to Crossley.

■ RIGHT *Avery manufactured gasoline tractors in Peoria, Illinois after switching from steam. Its largest machine was the four cylinder 40–80, one of a range of five models in 1919.*

■ LEFT *The Waterloo Boy Model N was the first tractor tested by the University of Nebraska in what became the noted Nebraska tractor tests. The company was later acquired by John Deere and helped to establish that company as a tractor maker.*

Other manufacturers were also developing tractors at this time, including Ransome's of Ipswich. Petter produced its Patent Agricultural Tractor in 1903. Marshall and Daimler built machines and looked for export sales. To this end a Marshall tractor was exhibited in Winnipeg, Canada in 1908.

In 1910 Werkhuizen Leon Claeys, founded in 1906, built its factory in Zedelgem, Belgium, to manufacture harvesting machinery. There were other, similar, tentative steps being made in numerous European countries. However, because labour was more plentiful and cheaper in Europe than in the United States, technological innovation was slower as it was not such an economic necessity. In Germany, Adolf Altona built a tractor powered by a single-cylinder engine that featured chain drive to the wheels. This machine was not wholly successful but considerable progress was made in Europe as a result of Rudolph Diesel's experiments with engines.

Diesel (1858–1913), sponsored by Krupp in Berlin, created a low-cost reliable engine that ultimately bore his name; it operated by compression-ignition and ran on heavy oil. Diesel experimented in France, England and Germany and found widespread acceptance of his engines throughout the world. He disappeared off a British cross-channel steamer during the night of 29 September 1913 and is believed to have committed suicide.

Deutz introduced a tractor and motor plough of what was considered to be an advanced design in 1907. Deutsche Kraftplug, Hanomag, Pohl and Lanz were four other German companies involved in the manufacture of tractors and powered agricultural machinery.

In France, De Souza and Gougis were two of the manufacturers that entered tractors in a tractor trial held at the National Agricultural College at Grignon, near Paris, where tractors undertook a variety of voluntary and

■ BELOW *While a number of tractor makers relied on an in-line four-cylinder engine configuration for their tractors Case persevered with Crossmotor models such as this 15–27 model of 1921.*

■ RIGHT *The merger of McCormick and Deering in 1902 led to the production of Mogul and Titan tractors for respective dealers of each make. This is a 1919 22hp Titan.*

compulsory tests. Elsewhere in Europe, progress was also being made. Munktell in Sweden made a tractor in 1913 and in Italy Pavesi made the Tipo B. In 1910, Giovanni Landini manufactured the first tractor with a fixed-mounted "hot-bulb" engine. In Russia an engineering company produced three designs prior to World War I.

Experimentation with tractors, crawler tracks and agricultural machinery continued until the outbreak of World War I. Farming had been depressed during this time, but the war demanded a huge jump in productivity. The British wartime government instituted policies

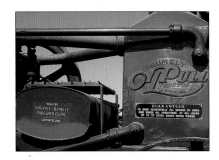

■ RIGHT *Advance-Rumely of LaPorte, Indiana was founded in 1915 and was one of the early tractor makers that was later absorbed into the Allis-Chalmers Company.*

to encourage increased domestic food production, including speeding up the rate of mechanization in an attempt to increase productivity and reduce the labour needed. A number of tractor producers had gone over to war-related work – Ruston Hornsby of Lincoln was involved with tank experimentation – but Saunderson tractors were in production and Weeks-Dungey entered the market in 1915.

Importing tractors from the United States was seen as a quick way to increase their numbers on British farms. The International Harvester Corporation marketed the models from its range that it considered to be most suited to British farming conditions: the Titan 10-20 and the Mogul 8-16. The Big Bull was marketed as the Whiting-Bull and a Parret model was renamed the Clydesdale. Another import was the Waterloo Boy, sold in Britain as the Overtime by the Overtime Farm Tractor Company. The Austin Motor Company offered a Peoria model and marketed it in Britain as the Model 1 Culti-Tractor. The war was to have far-reaching effects on both the economics of farming and on the production of tractors.

The Evolution of the Tractor

By the end of World War I, the tractor was generally accepted as being
a practical agricultural machine: Britain and the United States were exporting
machines around the globe to countries as distant as Russia, South America and
Australia. Henry Ford's mass-produced Fordson tractors, launched in 1917,
established themselves commercially; they were initially manufactured in the
United States for sale in Britain and beyond. The end of the war brought
irreversible socio-economic changes and this meant that agriculture became
increasingly mechanized as the 20th century progressed.

THE POST-WAR BOOM IN TRACTOR PRODUCTION

A period of prosperity followed World War I and in this boom the number of tractor manufacturers around the world quickly increased, while the tractor market shifted significantly. Acceptance of the fact that smaller tractors were practical changed the emphasis of the industry and threatened some of the established companies. Many of the new concerns were small companies with limited chances of success, especially when mass-produced machines, such as the Fordson, were gaining sales everywhere. Ford's tractor sold in vast numbers, achieving 75 per cent of total tractor sales in America. It was cheap to produce, so a greater number of farmers could afford it. Many small manufacturers struggled against this, producing insignificant numbers of various machines. They experimented and innovated but their products were never realistic long-term propositions.

By 1921 there were an estimated 186 tractor companies in business in the United States and production totalled 70,000 machines. There were also tractor producers in most European countries by the 1920s, including Breda, Pavesi, Fiat, Bubba and Landini in Italy, Steyr in Austria, Hofherr and Schrantz (HSCS) in Hungary, Hurliman and Burer in Switzerland and Kommunar in the USSR. Tractor makers in Australia included Ronaldson and Tippet. In the United States some of the small new companies included Bates, Ebert-Duryea,

■ ABOVE *Diesel engines became popular in European tractors after World War I. This 1930 Fendt Dieselross has a 1000cc Deutz single cylinder diesel engine.*

■ LEFT *Taken in 1993 this photograph shows Jessica Godwin at 101 years of age, reunited with Fordson tractor number one made in 1917 when she was 25.*

■ ABOVE *This 1928 Deutz tractor is fitted with a side mower, powered by a single cylinder engine of 800cc/50cu in displacement. It runs on benzine fuel.*

Fagiol, Kardell, Lang, Michigan and Utility. A representative European product of the period was the Glasgow tractor, named after the city in which it was built between 1919 and 1924. It was produced by the DL Company, that had taken over the lease of a former munitions factory after the Armistice. The Glasgow was a three-wheeled machine, arranged with two wheels at the front and a single driven wheel at the rear to eliminate the need for a differential. The design was typical of a number of budget

tractors built by small companies in both the United States and Europe.

Despite the influx of new manufacturers, the American tractor market soon developed into a competition for sales between Fordson, International Harvester, Case and John Deere. Fordson cut its prices to keep sales up, and in order to compete with the International Harvester Corporation offered a free plough with each tractor it sold. Having cleared all its outstanding stock with this marketing ploy, the

■ RIGHT *Large machines such as the Advance-Rumely Oil Pull 16–30 Model H became outdated during the 1920s, and were superseded by lighter, more compact, tractors.*

■ RIGHT *John Deere's Model D debuted in 1924 and production lasted until 1953, during which time more than 160,000 were manufactured. The GP was developed alongside the Model D intended for specific row crop cultivation.*

company was able to introduce its 15-30 and 10-20 models in 1921 and 1923 respectively, following these with the first proper row crop tractor in 1924. Called the Farmall, it was designed to be suitable for cultivation as it could be driven safely along rows of cotton, corn and other growing crops.

From then on the rival manufacturers used innovation as a way of staying ahead of the competition. Allis-Chalmers, Case, International Harvester, John Deere, Massey-Harris and Minneapolis-Moline all sought to offer more advanced tractors to their customers in order to win sales. For example, following Ford and International Harvester, Case introduced a cast frame tractor and although the engine ran across the frame, the model proved popular. Not to be outdone, John Deere offered its own interpretation of the cast frame tractor with the Model D of 1924. It was powered by a two-cylinder kerosene engine and had two forward gears and one reverse.

In Britain, the car maker Austin

manufactured a tractor powered by one of its car engines. It sold well despite competition from the Fordson and stayed in production for several years. Ruston of Lincoln and Vickers from Newcastle-upon-Tyne manufactured tractors and Clayton made a crawler tractor

■ ABOVE *Steam engines such as this Fowler ploughing engine of 1920 were gradually replaced by tractors that towed ploughs from the rear drawbar.*

■ LEFT *As well as towing farm implements the tractor was eminently suited to the belt driving of machinery, as this John Deere illustrates. Tractors were rated with both drawbar and belt hp.*

■ RIGHT *As a result of the pioneering work by Henry Ford, tractor production was soon carried out on assembly lines. This method of production spread to all manufacturers, including Ursus.*

■ FAR RIGHT *Centralized production and farming were among the corner-stones of Soviet policy and reached Poland in the aftermath of World War II.*

■ ABOVE *The German manufacturer, Lanz introduced the Bulldog tractor in 1921.*

but, as in America, the other manufacturers were continually competing against the volume, price and quality of the Fordson tractor. The 1929 transfer of all Ford tractor manufacturing to Cork in Ireland showed that there was, by now, much in common between the tractor industries on each side of the Atlantic. Five years earlier the low-priced Fordson Model F tractor had gone on sale in Germany, meaning that German manufacturers also had to compete with Ford. Despite the similarities in worldwide tractor manufacturing there were still differences: one was in the different types of fuel employed by Ford and the Germans.

German manufacturers such as Stock and Hanomag publicly compared the Fordson's fuel consumption unfavourably with that of their own machines that used diesel fuel. Lanz introduced its Feldank tractor, that was capable of running on low-grade fuel through use of a semi-diesel engine. The Lanz company later introduced the Bulldog which the company became noted for. The first Bulldog models were basic and in many ways not as advanced as the Fordson. The Lanz HL model had no reverse gear, and power came from a single horizontal cylinder, two-stroke, semi-diesel engine that produced 12hp.

THE NEBRASKA TRACTOR TESTS

The purpose of tractor trials was to evaluate tractor performance and allow realistic comparisons to be made between the various models and makes. The Canadian Winnipeg Trials of 1908 were a success and became a regular event, continuing until 1912. A small tractor trial was held in Britain in 1910 while in the United States trials were held in Nebraska. The Nebraska Tractor Tests became established as a yardstick for determining the relative capabilities of tractors, preventing their manufacturers from claiming unlikely abilities and inflated levels of performance.

The tests were instituted as a result of a member of the Nebraska State Legislature acquiring both Ford and Bull tractors. Ford tractors were made by a Minneapolis company which had formed the Ford Tractor Company using the name of one of their engineers, and had nothing to do with the famous Henry Ford. The tractor did not amount to much and the eminent Nebraskan customer, Wilmot F. Crozier of Polk County, was less than satisfied

■ BELOW *A 1948 John Deere Model, a version of the model introduced in 1934 which achieved 18.72 drawbar and 24.71 belt hp.*

with it, as he was with the Bull tractor that he had also purchased. Consequently, he sponsored a bill to make tractor testing mandatory in the state.

Starting in 1920 a series of tests was undertaken to examine horsepower, fuel consumption, and engine efficiency. There were also practical tests that gauged the tractor's abilities with implements on a drawbar. The tests were carried out at the State University in Lincoln, Nebraska. The law decreed that manufacturers must print all or none of the test results in their publicity material, ensuring that no one could publish the praise and delete the criticism. The Nebraska tests were noted for their fairness and authority and this led to their general acceptance far beyond the boundaries of the state.

The results of Nebraska Test Number 266 serve as an example to show the quality of the data supplied. A Massey-Harris Pacemaker made by Massey-Harris Company of Racine,

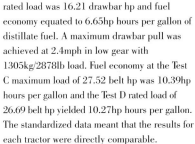

■ RIGHT *The Minneapolis-Moline U Models such as this 1942 UTS were introduced in 1938 and were rated at 30.86 drawbar and 38.12 belt hp in Nebraska tests.*

Wisconsin was tested between 10–19 August 1936. The tractor's equipment included a four-cylinder I-head Massey-Harris engine run at 1200rpm, with 9.84cm/3.875in bore and 13.3cm/5.25in stroke. It had an American Bosch U4 magneto, Kingston carburettor and a Handy governor. The tractor weighed 1837kg/4050lb. The Test H Data was as follows: in gear two a speed of 2.28kph/3.67mph was achieved, as was a load of 750kg/1658lb. The

■ LEFT *The belt drive pulley is seen here adjacent to the steering wheel on this International Harvester Corporation 8–16 Junior Model.*

■ BELOW *The horsepower rating was 8 drawbar hp and 16hp at the belt, hence the 8–16 designation.*

rated load was 16.21 drawbar hp and fuel economy equated to 6.65hp hours per gallon of distillate fuel. A maximum drawbar pull was achieved at 2.4mph in low gear with 1305kg/2878lb load. Fuel economy at the Test C maximum load of 27.52 belt hp was 10.39hp hours per gallon and the Test D rated load of 26.69 belt hp yielded 10.27hp hours per gallon. The standardized data meant that the results for each tractor were directly comparable.

Tractor trials were instituted at Rocquencourt, France in the spring of 1920. These tested both domestic and imported models as part of a government drive to mechanize farming in France. In the autumn of the same year further trials were held at Chartres and 116 tractors were entered, coming from 46 manufacturers from around the world. In Britain, tractor trials were inaugurated at Benson, Oxfordshire in 1930.

The first running of the event attracted a variety of interest from English and American tractor manufacturers, including Ford, whose Fordson tractors were at this time being made in Ireland. The British manufacturers who submitted machines included AEC Limited, Marshalls, Vickers, McClaren and Roadless. Tractors came from further afield too: an HSCS tractor manufactured in Hungary competed in the Benson trials.

THE ADVENT OF PNEUMATIC TYRES

One of the first men to experiment with pneumatic tyres was Charles Goodyear, a resident of Woburn, Massachusetts. In 1839 he purchased the patent rights to a sulphur treatment process that helped him in his development of vulcanization, which made rubber both elastic and non-sticking, thus rendering it suitable for use in pneumatic tyres. Goodyear died in 1860, leaving a rich legacy to the auto industry, but also thousands of dollars of debt incurred in the widespread promotion of his product. The first car built by Alexander Winton in 1896 ran on pneumatic tyres made by Benjamin Franklin Goodrich. These were the first pneumatic tyres manufactured in the United States. Eight years earlier, in Ireland, the pneumatic tyre had been rediscovered by John B. Dunlop. The pneumatic agricultural tyre was the next major advance in improved tractor technology. The lack of practical pneumatic tyres had, until the early 1930s, hampered the universal use of

tractors: while those with lugged metal wheels suitable for ploughing could not be used on surfaced public roads, solid tyres suitable for road use were inadequate in wet fields. Solid lugged wheels were also unsuitable for cultivation purposes, as they caused too much

■ ABOVE *This Farmall F-12 of the mid-1930s still has the old steel rimmed wheels that were in use before the advent of pneumatic tyres for tractors.*

■ LEFT *Pneumatic tyres were initially made available as an option in place of steel wheels, but soon became ubiquitous. They are fitted to this 1934 Farmall F-20.*

■ RIGHT *Like everything else connected with farming pneumatic tyres have become sophisticated, and various types and sizes are in use on this Massey Ferguson 6160 tractor and 139 baler.*

■ RIGHT *While Allis-Chalmers was the first to promote pneumatic tyres for tractors, other manufacturers quickly followed. Shown here is the Case 1938 Model R.*

■ BELOW *The advent of four-wheel drive and high-speed tractors has placed greater emphasis on the performance of pneumatic tyres, both in the field and on the road.*

damage to the roots of crops. In the United States, Goodrich experimented with a zero-pressure tyre while Firestone explored the use of modified aircraft tyres. These had moulded, angled lugs and were inflated to around 15psi, giving them enough flexibility to cope with uneven surfaces. In 1932 Allis-Chalmers Model U tractors fitted with aircraft-type tyres inflated to 15psi were successfully tested on a dairy farm in Waukesha, Wisconsin. The company used the new tyres on a tractor with a four-speed transmission capable of working at ploughing speeds and also achieved 24kph/15mph on the road. It advertised this achievement widely in the farming press, but also hired racing drivers to display its new

tractors with pneumatic tyres at speed, and unveiled a "hot rod" tractor at the Milwaukee State Fair of 1933. The tractor was shown working with a plough then a local racing driver, Frank Brisco, took it to 57kph/35.4mph on a race track. This created a sensation and Allis-Chalmers capitalized on the success by starting a tractor racing team. Valuable publicity was generated and by 1937 around 50 per cent of new tractors sold in the United States were fitted with pneumatic tyres.

Scientific tests on tractors fitted with pneumatic tyres showed that fuel economy improved. University of Iowa tests showed that although rubber tyres added around $200 to the price of a tractor it took as little as 500 hours' work to recover this additional outlay. Rubber tyres enhanced a tractor's versatility, making it more suited to road use, and before long manufacturers offered higher top gear ratios to allow faster highway travel.

THE SLIDE INTO DEPRESSION AND WORLD WAR II

The Wall Street Crash of 1929 and the economics of production and competition meant that the 1930s started on a different note to the previous decade. Gone was the optimism, and with it the numerous small tractor manufacturers with only a partially proven product. Only a few large companies remained producing fully workable tractors, whose new models reflected the increasing use of engineering technology. These included simple refinements such as the oil bath air filter, that gave engines a longer life when used in dusty conditions. Alongside these developments were improvements in vehicle lighting and fuel-refining techniques that enabled improvements in the efficiency and workability of tractors to be achieved. The Depression only slowed innovation rather than eliminating it, and it did not entirely deter new manufacturers from entering the market. In some countries the tractor-making companies had to take their chances in a competitive capitalist market, while in others there was less competition. In the USSR, created as a result of the Russian Revolution of 1917, tractor production continued under the auspices of the State.

■ ABOVE *As the tractor became more accepted and affordable it was not uncommon to see it being used with horses, as with this John Deere during harvesting.*

■ BELOW *The Depression reached its depths in 1932 but tractors were still being produced, as evidenced by this 1932 McCormick-Deering 10–20.*

Charles Deere Wiman, a great-grandson of John Deere, had taken over direction of the John Deere Company in 1928. Through the Great Depression, despite losses in the first three years of that decade, the company made a decision to support its debtor farmers as long as was necessary. The John Deere Company was fortunate that it had sufficient capital to be able to do this and was no doubt aware that it needed farmers to buy tractors as much as farmers depended on the machines.

During the worst of the Depression the total tractor production for 1932 was in the region of 20,000 and by 1933 only nine principal American manufacturers remained in the tractor business. These were Allis-Chalmers, Case, Caterpillar, Cleveland Tractor, International Harvester, John Deere, Massey, Minneapolis-Moline and Oliver. The Depression affected Europe equally badly but the major companies survived. In the years to come after World War II the tractor market would be divided between these makes, although mergers and amalgamations within the industry meant that numerous small tractor

■ LEFT *Despite worsening economic conditions International Harvester produced the 10–20 model while McCormick-Deering developed the similarly powered Farmall.*

■ RIGHT *The World War would necessitate intensified production of tractors in order to increase agricultural production.*

■ LEFT *Changing economic conditions caused Henry Ford to abandon tractor production in the United States in 1929 and transfer to Ireland, then England.*

■ RIGHT *Lanz tractors such as this 1923 12hp model, were basic and lacked reverse gears – the engine was simply run backwards to change direction.*

■ LEFT *The English Rushton tractor of the 1930s was closely modelled on the Fordson. This is a 14–20 four-cylinder model.*

makers, as well as makers of agricultural implements and specialized equipment, would eventually become constituent parts of the handful of global corporations manufacturing agricultural machinery. The tractor industry has, throughout its history, been characterized

■ BELOW *In the late 1920s Caterpillar introduced a series of smaller crawler machines aimed at farmers. This one is haymaking in England in the 1930s.*

by takeovers and mergers of both fledgling and established companies in the race for sales and technological advances.

Around the globe, in the shorter term, technological progress was made. In 1940 New Holland changed owners and, following a

■ LEFT *The Lanz Bulldog concept proved popular in Europe to the extent that it was manufactured by numerous other companies.*

■ BELOW *During World War II British women took over men's jobs. These women are using a Fordson tractor and reaper for haymaking.*

company reorganization, began production of the first successful automatic pick-up hay baler. A year earlier Harry Ferguson and Henry Ford had made an agreement to produce tractors together and the result was the Model 9N. The 9N was virtually a new design although it had some similarities with the Fergusons of the mid-1930s manufactured by David Brown.

When World War II broke out in Europe on 3 September 1939, there were three major tractor producers in business in Britain: Fordson, Marshall and David Brown. It was immediately clear that once again a larger number of tractors would be required if farmers were to be able to feed the nation through the oncoming war. It was also apparent that tractors (like much other war material) would have to be imported from the United States, initially as ordinary purchases and later by means of the lend-lease scheme. This meant that the major American tractor manufacturers would be supplying their products in considerable numbers. Allis-Chalmers, Case, John Deere, Caterpillar, Minneapolis-Moline, Massey-Harris, Oliver, International Harvester and Ford machines were all imported. Ford also continued production at its British factory and the machines were redesigned to use less metal, and painted to make them less obvious in fields. Two years later, in December 1941,

■ RIGHT *Hanomag was one of the German tractor-making companies that thrived during the 1930s with the production of both wheeled and tracked diesel engined machines.*

■ BELOW *Tractors found a wartime role on airfields. Here, a Fordson is seen towing a bomb trolley for the RAF Lancaster bomber seen behind its returning crew.*

America entered the war, with the Japanese airstrike on Pearl Harbor in Hawaii. The might of American industry was now dedicated to winning the war, but the wartime exports had popularized American tractor brands far beyond their place of manufacture.

■ LEFT *A 1934 MTZ 320 Deutz diesel tractor. Deutz, like Hanomag, specialized in diesel and semi-diesel engined tractor manufacture, as these engine types were favoured in parts of Europe.*

■ RIGHT *In the aftermath of World War I few tractor manufacturers existed in France although the likes of Latil, Renault and Austin did produce tractors there.*

■ LEFT *An earlier example of the Deutz diesel engined tractor which found favour in Europe prior to the outbreak of World War II. Steel wheels are indicative of the basic design.*

■ RIGHT *Before World War II, tractors were more stylishly advanced in America where, by 1934, the Model A was in production.*

Shortages caused by the war led to the modification of designs. The numerous Japanese conquests in the Far East resulted in a rubber shortage, for example, which meant that steel wheels came back into use. Pre-war designs became standardized and remained in production throughout the war period, with only minor and necessary changes being made. The changes could wait but the war years allowed the manufacturers to assist the war effort and plan for the post-war decades. John Deere's factories, for example, produced a wide range of war-related products, ranging from tank transmissions to mobile laundry units, but throughout this period, John Deere nonetheless maintained its emphasis on product design, and developed a strong position for the post-war market through the efforts of Charles Wiman and the wartime president, Burton Peek.

International Harvester and White manufactured half-tracks that were to provide the basis for a variety of special vehicles, including armoured personnel carriers, mortar carriers, self-propelled gun mounts and anti-aircraft gun platforms. Vast numbers were supplied under the lend-lease scheme to

Britain, Canada and Russia, and many of the machines produced by International Harvester went abroad in this manner. Massey-Harris made approximately 2,500 tanks for the US army. Case made 15,000 tractors specifically for the military out of a total of 75,000 made for the war effort. Case employees assisted the war effort in another way: volunteers from the factory formed the 518th Ordnance Company Heavy Maintenance US Army.

■ BELOW *Although this is an early Fordson, steel wheels became common again during World War II due to rubber shortages caused by Japanese conquests.*

The Innovators

The development of the tractor and other farming machinery was given additional impetus as a result of the efforts of numerous individuals in different countries. John Deere developed a steel plough suited for prairie use; later Henry Ford brought the capabilities of mass production to tractor manufacture; Messrs Holt and Best developed successful crawler technology; Jerome Case developed a workable thresher, and Cyrus McCormick a reaper. Adolphe Kégresse developed light crawlers with rubber tracks and later Harry Ferguson developed the three-point linkage for attaching implements to tractors. The sum of these men's efforts has led to the production of the technologically advanced tractors of today.

JOHN DEERE (1804–1886)

The story of John Deere, who developed the world's first commercially successful, self-scouring steel plough, closely parallels the settlement and development of the midwestern United States, an area that the homesteaders of the 19th century considered the golden land of promise.

John Deere was born in Rutland, Vermont on 7 February 1804. He spent his boyhood and young adulthood in Middlebury, Vermont where he received a common school education and served a four-year apprenticeship learning the blacksmith's trade. In 1825, he began his career as a journeyman blacksmith and soon became noted for his careful workmanship and ingenuity. His highly polished hay forks and shovels, especially, were in great demand throughout western Vermont, but business conditions in the state became depressed in the mid-1830s, and the future looked gloomy for the ambitious young blacksmith. Many natives of Vermont emigrated to the West, and the tales of golden opportunity that filtered back to Vermont so stirred John Deere's enthusiasm that he decided to dispose of his business and join the pioneers. He left his wife and family,

■ ABOVE *John Deere the blacksmith from Vermont, United States whose company is now the only tractor-making one to still have its founder's full name as its brand name.*

■ LEFT *John Deere developed the self-scouring plough and his successors developed tractors such as the GP models of the 1920s, seen here being used in the construction of a haystack.*

■ ABOVE LEFT *John Deere became a "full-line" agricultural product manufacturer, making ploughs as well as harvesting machinery. Recently the company has considerably diversified.*

■ ABOVE RIGHT *Row crop tricycle tractors, high crop clearance models and other specialist machines have long been produced by John Deere, enabling the company to stay at the forefront of agriculture.*

who were to join him later, and set out with a bundle of tools and a small amount of cash. After travelling many weeks by canal boat, lake boat and stagecoach, he reached the village of Grand Detour, Illinois, a place named after a river meander, that had been settled by pioneers from his native Vermont. The need for a blacksmith was so great that within a short time of his arrival in 1836 he had built a forge and was busy serving the community. There was a lot of general blacksmithing work to be done shoeing horses, and repairing ploughs and other equipment for the pioneer farmers. From them he learned of the serious problem

they encountered in trying to farm the fertile but heavy soil of the Midwest. The cast-iron ploughs they had brought with them were designed for the light, sandy New England soil. The rich midwestern soil clung to the plough bottoms and every few steps it was necessary to scrape the soil from the plough. This made ploughing a slow and laborious task. Many pioneers were discouraged and were considering moving on, or heading back east.

John Deere studied the problem and became convinced that a plough with a highly polished and properly shaped mouldboard and share ought to scour itself as it turned the furrow

■ RIGHT *John Deere became involved in the tractor-making business after acquiring the Waterloo Boy company in 1918. It then had to catch up with established makers such as Ford.*

■ LEFT *A photo that illustrates how far John Deere harvesting technology has come in the course of a century, from binder to combine harvester: a Sidehill 6600 model.*

slice. In an attempt to provide a practical solution to the problem he fabricated a plough incorporating these new ideas in 1837, using the steel from a broken saw blade.

The new plough was successfully tested on the farm of Lewis Crandall near Grand Detour. Deere's steel plough proved to be exactly what the pioneer farmers needed for successful farming in what was then termed "the West", though his contribution to the growth of American agriculture would in due course far exceed the development of a successful design for a steel plough.

As a result of economic constraints, including those of labour and manufacturing costs, it was the practice of the day for blacksmiths to make tools to order for customers. John Deere's bold initiative was to manufacture his ploughs before he had orders for them. He would produce a stock of ploughs and then take them into the country areas to be sold. This was a wholly new approach to manufacturing and selling in the pioneer days, and one that quickly spread the word of John Deere's self-polishing ploughs.

Despite this innovative approach, there were many problems involved in attempting to operate a manufacturing business on the frontier including a lack of banks, a poor transport network and, worst of all, a scarcity of steel.

■ BELOW *A pneumatic tyred John Deere seed drill behind a row crop tricycle tractor. It is planting four rows at once.*

As a result, John Deere's first ploughs had to be produced with whatever pieces of steel he could locate. In 1843, he arranged for a shipment of special rolled steel from England. It had to be shipped across the Atlantic by steamship, up the Mississippi and Illinois Rivers by packet boat, and overland by wagon 65km/40 miles to Deere's infant factory in Grand Detour. In 1846, the first slab of cast plough steel ever rolled in the United States was made for John Deere and shipped from Pittsburgh to Moline, Illinois, where it was ready for use in the factory Deere opened there in 1848, to take advantage of the water power and easy transport offered by the

■ RIGHT *More than
150 years after John
Deere developed the
self-scouring plough
that helped make
cultivation of the
prairies possible, his
name is still prominent
on the sides of tractors
such as this.*

Mississippi River. Within ten years of developing his prototype, John Deere was producing 1,000 ploughs a year. In the early years of his business, Deere laid down several precepts that have been followed faithfully ever since by the company he founded. Among them was an insistence on high standards of quality. John Deere vowed, "I will never put my name on a plough that does not have in it the best that is in me." In 1868, Deere's business was incorporated under the name Deere & Company. The following year John Deere's son,

Charles, who was later to succeed him as president, was elected vice-president and treasurer. One of his early partners chided him for constantly making changes in design, saying it was unnecessary because the farmers had to take whatever they produced. Deere's viewpoint was more far-sighted: if he did not improve and refine products, somebody else would. As a result the John Deere Company has continued to place a strong emphasis on product improvement, and consistently devotes a higher share of its income to research and development than many competitors. Its role as a significant force in the tractor industry began when it purchased the Waterloo Gasoline Engine Company in 1918, and produced its Model D in 1924.

■ RIGHT *Charles
Deere, the son of John
Deere, became vice-
president and Treasurer
of the company and later
succeeded his father as
president of the company.*

■ FAR RIGHT *One of
the innovations
successfully employed
by John Deere's
successors was that of
styling tractors. Henry
Dreyfuss styled the
range in the 1930s and
this design continued
into the 1950s.*

JEROME INCREASE CASE (1819–1891)

Jerome Increase Case founded the J. I. Case Company in Racine, Wisconsin in 1842 and soon gained recognition as the first builder of a steam engine for agricultural use. During his tenure as president of the company, it manufactured more threshing machines and steam engines than any other company in history. In addition to his innate talents as an inventor and manufacturer, Case also took an interest in politics and finance. He was made mayor of Racine, serving for three terms, and he was also returned as state senator for the Racine area for two terms. He was the incorporator and president of the Manufacturer's National Bank of Racine and founder of the First National Bank of Burlington (Wisconsin). Case also founded the Wisconsin Academy of Science, Arts and Letters, was president of the Racine County Agricultural Society and president of the Wisconsin Agricultural Society. He was often referred to in manufacturing and agricultural

circles as the "Threshing Machine King". Case received a different kind of recognition as the owner of "Jay-Eye-See" (the phonetic rendering of his initials) – a black gelding racehorse acknowledged as the world's all-time champion trotter-pacer.

■ ABOVE *The company founded by J. I. Case became noted for the manufacture of threshing machines and later steam traction engines. Mass tractor manufacture was not started until 1911.*

■ LEFT *The company found itself in the doldrums in the mid-1930s and the sales people believed they could only sell the CC models, such as this, if IH dealers had sold all their F-12 models.*

At an early age, Jerome Case is said to have been inspired by an article in an agricultural newspaper about a new machine that would thresh wheat. For the farmer of the early 19th century, little had changed since biblical times: he cut wheat with a scythe, threshed it by hand with a flail and winnowed the grain from the chaff by tossing it in the air. It was back-breaking and time-consuming work. Each worker could thresh only six or seven bushels a day, thereby creating a bottleneck that prevented farmers from expanding the size and productivity of their holdings. Manpower in this period in the United States was relatively scarce. In 1820, the year after Case's birth, the population was about 5.5 million, although this figure did not include slaves. The further west one travelled the fewer people there were, so that farmers on the frontiers could count on little more than their own families as their workforce, which was one reason why farm families tended to be large. Case was born and lived during a pivotal period for Americans, when the technological achievements of the

■ ABOVE *The Case LA was a redesigned version of the Model L tractor. Its more rounded lines reflected the increasing emphasis on the appearance of tractors.*

Industrial Revolution were underpinning the expansion of the United States. He was to become a part of this process, along with other innovators such as Cyrus McCormick and Eli Whitney whose inventions transformed American agriculture. By applying ingenuity and technology to farming, these men so raised production levels that North America would become the breadbasket of the world.

Case began his business by refining a crude threshing machine in Rochester, Wisconsin; soon afterwards he moved to Racine to take advantage of the area's plentiful supply of water to power his machines. By 1847 he had constructed the three-storey premises which

■ LEFT *Case introduced the row crop Model CC tractor in 1930. The machines were painted grey, and had a distinctive side steering arm which was variously nicknamed the "chicken perch" and the "fence cutter".*

■ RIGHT *Case introduced a bright new hue for its tractors in 1939 with the R-series of tractors. The new colour was called Flambeau Red and was one of a number of refinements to the range.*

became the centre of his agricultural machinery business. At this time a horse-driven J. I. Case threshing machine retailed at between $290 and $350.

Case's business prospered to the extent that by 1848 it became, and remains, the largest employer in Racine. As the business grew, Case continued to develop his threshing machines. In 1852 he wrote to his wife after demonstrating one of them to a group of farmers, "All were united in saying that if the machine could thrash 200 bushels in a day it could not be equalled by any in the country." In the afternoon of the demonstration he hitched up the horses and, in half a day, "thrashed and cleaned 177 bushels of wheat".

By 1862 Case's threshers were much improved and a system known as the "Mounted Woodbury" was employed to power them. Horses were hitched in pairs to long levers that looked like huge spokes on a horizontally positioned wheel. The driver stood on a central platform to drive the horses and the power they generated was carried through a set of gears to long rods that drove the gears of the thresher. One machine so equipped was the Sweepstakes thresher – the first of Cases's named threshers – a machine capable of threshing up to 300 bushels a day.

■ ABOVE *The VA series of tractors, still in Flambeau Red, were introduced by Case in 1942 with the intention of increasing profitability by manufacturing more parts in-house.*

■ BELOW *Although J. I. Case built his business on threshers it is unlikely that he envisaged that machines such as this, seen here harvesting maize in Zambia, would bear his name.*

In 1863 Jerome Case formed a partnership, J. I. Case and Company, with Massena Erskine, Robert Baker and Stephen Bull. Two years later the firm adopted Old Abe as its mascot. Old Abe was a bald eagle that had been the mascot of Company C of the 8th Wisconsin Regiment during the American Civil War. In this year the Eclipse thresher was introduced. This was a further improved version of the earlier models, designed to provide a cleaner separation of grain and straw and cope with larger capacities of wheat.

Steam power was the next major innovation to be embraced by J. I. Case and Company. The first Case steam engine was constructed in 1869 and was the first of approximately 36,000 to be built. The early models were stationary engines, mounted on a chassis and pulled by horses. The engine was used simply to provide power for belt-driven implements such as threshers. By 1876 the company was building self-propelled steam traction engines, one of which won a Gold Medal for Excellence at the Centennial Exposition in Philadelphia. In this year the company sold 75 steam engines and in the following year increased this figure to 109.

In 1878 steam engine sales more than doubled and in that year Case's first export sale was made at the Paris Exposition.

In 1880 the J. I. Case and Company partnership was dissolved and the J. I. Case Threshing Machine Company was incorporated in its place. Refinements to the line of threshers were being made continually and in 1880 the much refined Agitator thresher was introduced, using an improved method of horse propulsion, namely the "Dingee Sweep" horse power. The company diversified into the manufacture of steam engines to power sawmills.

A story from 1884 gives an indication of Jerome Case's character. The company had sold a thresher to a Minnesota farmer and it was in need of repairs which the local dealer and a mechanic were unable to carry out. Jerome Case himself travelled to the farm to inspect the disabled thresher. A crowd, surprised by his visit and the distance he had travelled, watched as he attempted to repair the machine. He was unable to remedy the fault and was so concerned that a defective machine had left his factory that he burned the thresher to the ground. The following day a brand new Case thresher was delivered to the farm.

■ ABOVE *A Case tractor collecting mown grass for silage on an English farm. Case acquired the noted English tractor maker David Brown during 1972.*

■ BELOW *The Case DEX was especially manufactured for the British tractor market. As with the LA the final drive was by means of enclosed chains instead of gears.*

In 1885 Case, by now the largest steam engine maker in the world, looked towards the growing South American market and appointed a distributor for its west coast. This was followed by the opening of a Buenos Aires office in 1890. Jerome Case died in 1891 and his brother-in-law, Stephen Bull, became the company's president. In his lifetime Jerome Case had made an invaluable contribution to the mechanizing of agriculture and a line of farm machinery – Case IH – still bears his name to this day.

CYRUS HALL MCCORMICK (1809–1884)

The International Harvester Corporation was formed in 1902 through the merger of the McCormick and Deering companies. However, Cyrus McCormick's involvement with agriculture had begun in Rockbridge County, Virginia in 1831, when he demonstrated his grain reaper which was an improvement on ideas tried earlier by his father, Robert McCormick. Cyrus McCormick had patented his reaper by 1834 and sold one by 1840. It was a major step in the mechanization of the grain-harvesting process. The mechanical reaper obviated the need for endless hours of scything and trebled the output of even the

best farm labourer with a scythe. The new machines meant that productivity could be increased massively.

Having proven the reaper in Virginia, Cyrus McCormick moved west because, like Jerome Case and John Deere, he was aware of the potentially massive agricultural market on the

■ LEFT *Cyrus Hall McCormick, whose involvement with agricultural machinery went back to 1831, when he demonstrated his improved grain reaper in Virginia.*

■ FAR LEFT *By the time the merger between McCormick's and Deering's companies was being worked out in 1902, the gasoline tractor was already a practical machine.*

■ BELOW *Pneumatic tyres and row crop machines were still to be developed at the time of the merger, but the company would survive against Henry Ford's price cutting.*

■ ABOVE *The simple design of drawbar allowed the draft of numerous implements, especially ploughs and harvesting tools.*

■ ABOVE *From early in its distinguished history the McCormick-Deering IH company relied on overseas sales and manufacture. These tractors and implements are awaiting sale in France.*

prairies. McCormick established a plant to manufacture reapers in Chicago, Illinois in 1847. Production was soon under way and McCormick's brothers, Leander and William, joined him in the blossoming business. The demand for reapers ensured that the company flourished and the brothers prospered.

William died in 1865 and in 1871 the company's plant was burned down. The firm struggled as a result of this catastrophe but,

despite a financial loss, built a new factory on a larger site. In 1879 the company was incorporated as the McCormick Harvesting Machine Company. Cyrus was the second brother to die, in 1884. Six years later Nancy McCormick, his widow, and his son Cyrus Jr, bought the shares held by Leander McCormick. Cyrus Jr went on to head the McCormick Harvesting Machine Company successfully for several years.

■ RIGHT *Tractor design generally follows trends: having become more rounded in the post-war years, it again became more angular during the 1960s and 1970s.*

■ RIGHT *A classic F-Series Farmall tractor at a vintage tractor rally in the United States. It has the front wheels positioned close together in the standard tricycle row crop configuration.*

■ BELOW *A farmer seated on his International Harvester tractor against the blue sky of Nebraska.*

The company had a policy of buying patents that appeared to have potential, as well as making developments of its own, and so held its own against rival companies. The biggest rival faced by the McCormick concern was the Deering Harvester Company. As recently as 1870 William Deering, a successful businessman from Maine, had invested in the company which made the Marsh Harvester, a forerunner of the corn binder, patented by the brothers Charles and William Marsh in Illinois in 1858. The company prospered and by 1880 William Deering had become the owner of what was now known as the Deering Harvester

■ BELOW *The names McCormick, Deering, International Harvester and Farmall all appear on this tractor. IH owned McCormick-Deering, and Farmall was the name of the series of tractors.*

Company. As the years went by the two companies became embroiled in a sales war. Deering tried to sell his company to McCormick in 1897 but no agreement could be reached. Five years later a merger plan was worked out that combined the assets of both McCormick and Deering as well as some smaller companies. The new company was to be known as International Harvester and was massive by the standards of the day, being estimated to be worth approximately $120 million.

The new corporation set out to expand and did so considerably by exporting to much of the British Empire and beyond. A new factory was constructed in Hamilton, Ontario and other companies were purchased, including the Osborne Company, Weber Wagon Company, Aultman-Miller and the Keystone Company. This increased both the size of the operation and the number of product lines offered. As early as 1905 the company made inroads into Europe, building a plant in Norrkopping, Sweden and followed this with plants in Germany and Russia. Not for nothing had it prefixed its name with "International".

■ ABOVE *The Farmall Model M was one of three new models that made its debut in 1939 having been comprehensively styled by the noted industrial designer Raymond Loewy.*

■ BELOW *Tractor cabs were an innovation that were slow in coming despite Minneapolis-Moline's experimentation. Modern tractor cabs are now soundproofed and dustproofed.*

DANIEL BEST

Daniel Best was born in Ohio on 28 March 1838, the ninth child of 16 from his father's two marriages. As a youngster he lived for a time in Missouri, where his father ran a sawmill, before the family moved to Vincennes, Iowa to farm 400 acres. An older brother had already made the move to the West and encouraged Daniel to do the same. In 1859 he did so, working as a guard on a wagon train, and for the next ten years he earned a living in a variety of ways, mostly connected with the mining and timber industries.

During a spell working with his brothers, who produced corn in California, he designed and built a transportable machine for cleaning grain. The brothers operated the machine during the 1870 harvest season, and were able to clean up to 60 tons of grain per day. Best patented his machine in 1871 and entered a partnership with L. D. Brown; in the same year "Brown and Best's unrivalled seed separator" won first prize at the California State Fair. Best went on to patent a seed-coating machine and then a clothes-washing machine. He continued to dabble in the corn separator market,

especially when Oregon mandated that grain be cleaned before sale or transport. He went into partnership with Nathaniel Slate in Albany, Oregon and they opened a branch of their business in Oakland, California, choosing the location because it was a shipping port for grain and wheat as well as being a broker's market. Best then moved with his family to Washington to pursue more mining and timber interests.

The demand for Best's inventions continued to grow and he manufactured a variety of machines aimed at increasing productivity as well as mechanizing farming. Because of the growth in his business Best felt obliged to acquire larger premises. He sold some of his other interests in Washington and Oregon and bought the San Leandro Plow Company from Jacob Price. Renaming the concern the Daniel Best Agricultural Works, he moved production to San Leandro from both Albany and Oakland. At this time he also patented a combined header and thresher and a fan blast governor that allowed the machine to work at a constant speed regardless of variations in the speed at which it moved across the field. This innovation was acknowledged as a major step

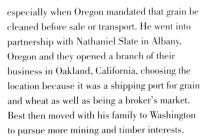

■ ABOVE *Daniel Best's patents left him in a position to charge a licence fee to other crawler manufacturers.*

■ BELOW *The Best 60 crawler was among the first machines to take crawler technology into the fields.*

■ RIGHT *Following the merger of Holt and Best, the new company's tractors became known as caterpillars. This is a 1929 model 30.*

towards quality control in grain harvesting and cleaning, as well as combining the two functions into a single machine. Over the next few years Best's company sold 150 of the machines to farmers in the states of Oregon, California and Washington.

■ BELOW *The 1939 caterpillar R2 is powered by a 25–31hp gasoline engine.*

The difference between Californian farms and those of the Midwest was their size. Most Californian wheat farms were much bigger and harvesting was a major labour-intensive task: some farms required the services of 150 horses. Best was of the opinion that the technology existed to mechanize the harvesting in order to save both man- and horsepower. That technology was steam power, which was already extant in two forms for agricultural use: the horse-drawn steam engine as a source of power and the self-propelled steam traction engine.

Best bought the rights to manufacture the Remington "Rough and Ready", a patented steam traction engine proven in both agricultural and logging applications. He went a step further than the blacksmith Remington had done, and contrived to make it both tow his combine harvester and power its auxiliary engine. He was successful and patented the machinery in 1889.

CHARLES HENRY HOLT

Charles Henry Holt was born in Loudon, New Hampshire. He went to school in Boston, where he subsequently studied accountancy. After periods working in his family's business, and then in the accounts department of a New York shipping company, he embarked on a ship in 1865 and sailed to San Francisco. He gained employment teaching and book-keeping some distance north of the city. Within two years he had amassed $700 and returned to San Francisco with ambition.

His family was in the timber business back in Concord, New Hampshire. They specialized in the supply of hardwoods used in the construction of wheels and wagons, so Charles Holt established himself, as C. H. Holt & Co, by buying timber from his father and selling it to Californian wagon and boat builders. There was considerable demand for this service because of the scale of developments then taking place in California. One of his brothers,

■ ABOVE *The Caterpillar D2 diesel was manufactured between 1938 and 1947 with only minor upgrades to the design.*

Frank, also moved out to California and established a branch of the business to produce wheels and their respective components. This was not entirely successful as the wheels made in the wetter atmosphere of the east were not suitable for the much drier western summers

■ ABOVE *The Caterpillar diesel 40 is powered by a 55hp 3-cylinder diesel engine. It is seen here in highway yellow, the trademark colour adopted by the company to replace the previously used grey.*

■ LEFT *A 1935 Caterpillar 28. It produced 37hp at the belt pulley when tested at Nebraska.*

■ RIGHT *A Caterpillar 2 ton. On the early models such as this the Caterpillar brand name is arranged to resemble a caterpillar insect.*

and frequently failed. To try to overcome this problem, wood was shipped to California and seasoned before being made into wheels, but this, too, was not wholly successful and the brothers looked for a place where the climate was more suited to their particular needs. They settled on Stockton, 150km/90 miles inland from San Francisco and formed the Stockton Wheel company. After around 60 years of successful manufacture of steam engines, and

some of the first viable crawlers, the Holt and Best companies merged to form the Caterpillar Tractor Company in 1925.

In 1931 the first Diesel Sixty Tractor rolled off the new assembly line in East Peoria, Illinois, with a new efficient source of power for track-type tractors. By 1940 the Caterpillar product line included motor graders, blade graders, elevating graders, terracers and electrical generator sets.

■ BELOW *A Caterpillar tractor exported to England to assist with the war effort.*

HENRY FORD (1863–1947)

Henry Ford was born on his father's farm near Dearborn, Michigan in 1863. He grew up with the drudgery of farm work and horse-drawn implements and it was this experience that fuelled his interest in things mechanical. By 1893 Ford was an engineer and an employee of the Edison Illuminating Company in Detroit, Michigan. In his spare time he experimented with internal combustion engines and their potential for vehicles. Henry Ford completed his first four-wheeled vehicle, a twin-cylinder, four-stroke engined, gasoline-fuelled quadricycle, on 4 June 189○ It had two forward gears and was c○ bie of 16kph/10mph in low and 32kph/20mph in high. The ex-farmer and skilled mechanic went on to build another car while still in Thomas Edison's employ – this was the "autobuggy", a tiller-steered two-cylinder car with planetary gear transmission and chain drive.

In 1899 he left the Edison Illuminating Company and founded the Detroit Auto

Company, that was initially heavily involved in car racing. It metamorphosed into the Henry Ford Company, which Ford later left after a disagreement about the direction that the company should take: he wanted to build

■ ABOVE *Henry Ford sitting in one of his experimental automobiles constructed while he was still in the employ of the Edison Illuminating Company.*

■ LEFT *The Fordson E27N was a tractor manufactured at a Ford plant in Dagenham, England. It was a development of the World War II era when Fordson had contributed to Britain's war effort.*

Motor Company. Ford's Model A was staked as the equivalent of $25,000 and in the next few months 1708 of them were sold at $850 each. In 1905 the Society of Automobile (later Automotive) Engineers was formed and Henry Ford was elected as one of the vice-presidents. This was at a time when the proponents of steam and electric cars were falling by the wayside and the internal combustion engine was becoming dominant. In the 1906–7 sales year Ford became the world's largest car maker with the manufacture of 8423 four-cylinder 15hp Model N cars selling at $550 each. Ford owned 51 per cent of the company's stock and the company made a profit of $1 million. Henry Ford's reputation was assured.

In the same year Ford turned his attention to the possibility of making tractors and assembled a prototype with a view to building the world's first mass-produced agricultural tractor. It was based around the engine and transmission from a 1903 Model B car. Experimentation continued until 1915, when Henry Ford announced that his first tractor would be a light two-plough tractor that would sell for $200. His aim was to do for farmers with an affordable tractor what his affordable

low-cost, affordable machines while his colleagues wanted to build luxury motorcars. After his departure, the company was re-formed as the Cadillac Company.

In 1902, Ford built an experimental people's car and in June 1903 he and 12 other men raised capital of $100,000 and set up the Ford

■ RIGHT *These tractors are harvesting in the Rusitu Valley, Zimbabwe. Ford tractors were later given a distinctive blue livery which made them recognizable all over the world.*

cars had done for motoring in general.

While development of the tractors was under way Henry Ford did not neglect car production or his workforce. In January 1914 he guaranteed that wages of not less than $5 per day would be paid to non-salaried employees and that there would be a profit-sharing scheme. In August he announced to the motoring public that if the company sold more than 300,000 Model T Fords in the next twelve months he would rebate up to $60 on the price paid. As a result, production soared to three times that of his competitors. The company had a dividend of $12.2 million in the next year and the employees divided up a $10 million bonus. In 1915, as he had promised, he refunded $50 to the purchasers of Model T Fords, having exceeded the 300,000 figure. The company made its millionth car in this year, with the Model T retailing at $440. The Model T was by this time so ubiquitous that a number of companies, such as the Pulford Company of Quincy, Illinois, offered axle conversions to enable the car to be used as a tractor to pull ploughs and harrows. Another similar conversion was offered by Eros.

In 1917 Ford was preparing to assemble his new tractors in Britain, but the pressures of the war meant that production had to be transferred to the United States instead. Within four months the Fordson Model F was being produced. The design appeared unconventional in an era of large tractors and three-wheeled machines. It was powered by an in-line, four-cylinder, gasoline engine and used the magneto ignition system of the Model T Ford car. However, the reputation of Ford's automobiles ensured that the new tractor would be taken seriously. Sales achieved a total in excess of 34,000 in 1918 and increased exponentially.

Ford produced tractors that were reliable and incorporated refinements gradually as technology advanced. As early as 1918 the Fordson had a high tension magneto, a water pump and an electric starter. Ford continued to make the Fordson Model F during the 1920s and sold the model in numbers commensurate with the recession. This period saw Fordson engaged in a sales war with the International Harvester Corporation. Cutting prices was one tactic and moving production was another. Production of tractors by Fordson in the United States ended in 1928 but it continued elsewhere, including Ireland and England.

The next step was to introduce even more innovative but affordable tractor technology.

■ ABOVE *Mass production of tractors by companies including Ford has led to the mechanization of farming in most countries around the world, regardless of the crop type.*

■ RIGHT *A Ford tractor with the distinctive blue oval logo at work on a coffee plantation in Zambia. The driver is wearing protective clothing.*

■ BELOW *A Ford tractor being used in conjunction with the development of arable crop cultivation in Luanshya, Zambia.*

Henry Ford made a deal with Harry Ferguson, which was sealed with only a handshake. Ferguson had invented the three-point hitch and Ford agreed to put it on his new Ford 9N tractor. This innovative technology endeared Ford's tractors, and in particular the Model 9N, to his farming customers. This was one of Ford's last major achievements in agricultural technology. He died on 7 April 1947 and his grandson, Henry Ford II, assumed charge of the company. It is impossible to quantify the impact Henry Ford had, not just on the tractor industry with the 1.5 million tractors made by his company in his lifetime, but on industry as a whole with his pioneering of mass production and assembly line techniques.

ADOLPHE KÉGRESSE

Half-track crawler technology was conceived as a way of keeping vehicles mobile away from surfaced roads, where more conventional wheeled vehicles soon became bogged down. Its history extends as far back as the early decades of the 20th century. In the United States and Europe manufacturers sought to produce useful half-tracks, mainly for agricultural work. Holt, Nash and Delahaye were three such companies but their machines tended to be slow and cumbersome.

The breakthrough was achieved in France during the early 1920s as a result of the efforts of Adolphe Kégresse. Kégresse, a Frenchman, worked for the Russian royal family as technical manager of the imperial garages. Around 1910, the Tsar wanted to follow a winter hunt in one of his motorcars and would not accept Kégresse's argument that the idea was impractical. Kégresse drove one of the cars into the snow, embedded it in a snowdrift and produced photographs of the stranded car for the Tsar. To overcome the problem, Kégresse began to work on a system of continuous rubber tracks running on light bogies that

■ ABOVE *One of the Citroën Kégresse machines built specially for the successful 1922-3 crossing of the Sahara desert.*

■ BELOW *Adolphe Kégresse developed his half-track system in the Russian snow for Tsar Nicholas II.*

would give a car mobility in snow. His system was a success and he converted the Packard and Rolls Royce cars belonging to Tsar Nicholas II to improve their performance in the snow. Subsequently, Austin armoured cars were also converted.

Following the Russian Revolution of 1917, Kégresse fled home to France via Finland. He left behind him about a dozen almost-completed converted cars, which were seized by the Bolsheviks and employed in military actions against the Polish. The Polish army captured one and despatched it to Paris, where it was examined by the French army.

In Paris, the industrialists André Citroën and M. Hinstin became interested in Kégresse's system. In 1921 the first "Autochenille" was manufactured based around a Citroën 10 CV Model B2 car. The Kégresse-Hinstin bogies pivoted on the driven rear axle to which they were fitted in place of wheels. An important difference between Kégresse crawler tracks and those used on tanks at the time was that the former were made from rubber and

canvas. The advantage of this was lightness of weight and considerable flexibility, which ensured that the tracks followed every contour of the ground. The tracks were fitted with rubber teeth on the inside to engage with the pulleys. Experimentation had proved that steel teeth were prone to collecting snow, which was packed into the joints by movement until the tracks stretched beyond breaking point. The snow did not adhere to the rubber teeth.

Tests of the new vehicle were carried out in the snow of the French Alps and the innovative development was greeted with acclaim. Adolphe Kégresse went to work for André Citroën, who was fascinated by the potential of this development. The Swiss post office was one of Citroën's customers for the Autochenille, and its vehicles were equipped with skis at the front.

Citroën was of the opinion that if the machines were effective in snow they would work equally well in sand and loose stones. In the winter of 1921–2 trials took place in the deserts of North Africa and a few improvements were made as a result of this testing. The developed half-tracks earned a formidable reputation and widespread publicity when the first motor vehicle crossing of the Sahara Desert was carried out by a team driving five Kégresse machines. They were equipped with additional radiators and used aluminium in their construction to minimize weight. Power came from 1452cc/88.5cu in engines with a bore and stroke of 68 x 100mm/2.68 x 3.94in driving through a three-speed transmission. The back axle was a two-speed unit, thereby increasing the range of the three-speed transmission, and enabling the machines to deal with varied terrain. The Autochenilles

■ RIGHT *Adolphe Kégresse demonstrating the cross-country prowess of one of his converted Citroën machines with a general-purpose trailer.*

■ LEFT *As well as in the sand the Citroën half-track system excelled in snow, as here in the Alps.*

were capable of a maximum speed of 45kph/28mph. The 3,600km/2,250 mile trip took place between December 1922 and January 1923 and was led by Georges Marie Haardt, Citroën's managing director, and Louis Audouin Dubreuil, a man with considerable experience of the Sahara. Nine other men, including five Citroën mechanics, and a dog, Flossie, accompanied the vehicles. With relatively few problems the team made the crossing to Timbuktu. Haardt and Dubreuil together also led a Central Africa Expedition, the Croisiäre Noire, from Algeria to the Cape between November 1924 and July 1925.

The British experimented with the Kégresse system and installed bogies on Crossley lorry chassis, of both 1270kg/25cwt and 1524kg/30cwt capability. In Italy, Alfa Romeo built an experimental Kégresse crawler tractor that could be driven in either direction as it was equipped with two steering wheels and two driver's seats. The Kégresse system of endless rubber band tracks was a success from the start and soon there was demand for a heavier duty version of the system. Adolphe Kégresse redesigned the components, refining his idea considerably, and produced the new version with a completely new style of bogie. It differed from the original in that the driven axle was now at the front of the track and was fitted with sprockets rather than relying on friction. Citroën, Panhard, Somua and Unic all used the new design on vehicles throughout the 1930s. Somua built the MCL and MCG half-track tractors with four-cylinder petrol engines that produced 60bhp at 2000rpm. The company also produced the S-35 cavalry tank and the AMR Gedron-Somua armoured car. Unic built

■ ABOVE *The advantages of Kégresse's rubber tracks were immediately apparent in heavy soil conditions such as those experienced here.*

the Model P107 artillery tractor. In Poland, Polski-Fiat built their Model 621L with Kégresse bogies while in Britain Burford-Kégresse produced the MA 3 ton machine and in Belgium FN manufactured Kégresse-equipped machines. Most of these were used

primarily as gun tractors. A third Kégresse-borne expedition in 1931 took French crews in seven half-tracks from Beirut to French Indochina (now Vietnam) between April 1931 and March 1932. A Kégresse P17 half-track was shipped from France to the United States for testing and evaluation in May 1931. Cunningham, Son and Company of Rochester, New York built their version, the T1, and in 1933 the Rock Island Arsenal built 30 of an upgraded model, the T1E1. This in turn led to the International Harvester half-track by the end of the 1930s. Although he was not as directly involved with agriculture as some of the other innovators, Adolphe Kégresse made a substantial contribution to the development of crawler track technology around the world. It is noteworthy that the most modern agricultural crawler tractors use rubber tracks like those pioneered by Kégresse.

■ RIGHT *A Kégresse converted machine being used to power a binder during an English harvest in the 1920s.*

HARRY FERGUSON (1884–1960)

Harry Ferguson was the son of an Irish farmer. He was still a young man when he showed a flair for mechanics and engineering. During his early twenties, he worked for his brother as a mechanic and a race pilot. Later, he designed and built several aeroplanes which he piloted. He became the Belfast agent for Overtime tractors (Waterloo Boy models renamed for the British market) and this first experience with tractors, together with a spell working for the Irish Board of Agriculture, started him thinking of better ways of attaching implements. After researching agriculture and, in particular, tractors and ploughs, he devised a two-bottom plough to be directly attached to a Model T Ford car. It was raised and lowered by a lever and, unlike other similar conversions available at the time, was simple to operate and did not

■ ABOVE *An enamelled lapel badge made to promote the Ferguson System used on Ferguson tractors in the aftermath of Harry Ferguson's split with Henry Ford.*

■ LEFT *Harry Ferguson, the Irish engineer who developed the acclaimed three-point hitch, which changed the face of farming and led to the manufacture of an eponymous range of tractors.*

■ BELOW *A Massey-Ferguson tractor in use in the village of Baaseli in the Rajasthan State of India.*

require wheels or a drawbar. Ferguson later developed a plough suitable for use with the Fordson Model F tractor. His first system was devised from a series of springs and levers. In 1925, with Eber and George Sherman in the United States, he founded Ferguson-Sherman Inc which produced a plough with the "Duplex" hitch system compatible with Fordson line tractors. He made his first Ferguson hydraulic system for his prototype tractor, for which the British David Brown Company had made the differential gear and transmission. In 1933, in partnership with David Brown, Harry Ferguson founded the Ferguson-Brown Company. The result was 1,250 Ferguson-Brown Model A tractors. All of these were equipped with the Ferguson hydraulic system. After this, Ferguson and Brown went separate ways as they had different ideas about the direction the development of tractors should take.

In 1938, Harry Ferguson met Henry Ford and as a result of their so-called "handshake agreement" Ford was able to produce Ferguson System tractors. Both parties brought different assets to the agreement: Henry Ford's reputation and manufacturing capacity were involved as well as an important part of his financial resources. Harry Ferguson brought

■ ABOVE *Following the split with the Ford company Harry Ferguson began manufacture of the TE20, seen here, ploughing, in England.*

■ RIGHT *The TE20 was similar in design to the Ford 9N but differed in that it had a four-speed transmission and an overhead valve engine.*

■ BELOW *In the UK mass production of the TE20 was carried out by the Standard Motor Company, and production frequently exceeded 500 tractors per week.*

the patents for the innovative ploughing system which offered Ford an advantage in his ongoing sales war with International Harvester.

Called the Ferguson System, the three-point hitch was put together using a combination of linkages, three different linkage points – two on the bottom and another one on the top – and hydraulics. Hooking up an implement to a tractor had previously been a complicated affair. Farmers used hoists, helpers, jacks and all kinds of imaginative ways to get heavy implements hooked up. With the Ferguson System they needed only to back up to the implement, hook it up, raise it on the linkage and drive off. The Ferguson System was used on Ford's 9N and

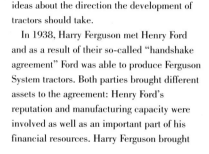

■ LEFT *In Britain the
TE20 became
affectionately known as
the "Grey Fergy". The
number produced and
reputation for reliability
has ensured that many,
including these two,
have been preserved.*

2N Models. At the same time, through Harry
Ferguson Inc, Ferguson continued to sell
tractors, parts and equipment, including several
machines produced by Ferguson-Sherman Inc.
Towards the end of 1946, Henry Ford's grandson,
Henry Ford II, advised Harry Ferguson that
his agreement with Ford would be ending on
30 June 1947. Ford then introduced a new
model, the Fordson 8N, that had similarities
with the Ford-Ferguson 2N.

When the Ford Motor Company started to
sell its new model, Harry Ferguson took two
courses of action. First, he commenced
litigation, pursuing the Ford Motor Company
and its associates for millions of dollars.
Second, he negotiated with the Standard
Motors Company in Britain for it to produce his
own tractor, the Model TE20 (TE was an
acronym for "Tractor England"). This was
similar to the Ford Models 9N and 2N.
Nonetheless, it differed from the 9N in having
a four-speed gearbox, an overhead valve
engine, two foot-operated brake pedals on the
left side and a one-piece bonnet (hood).
Ferguson drove his first Model TO20 ("Tractor
Overseas"), built in Detroit, in 1948.

The Models TO20 and TE20 were identical
except for their electrical systems and
transmission cases. The TO20 had a Delco
electrical system and a cast-iron transmission
case, whereas the TE20 had a Lucas electrical
system and an aluminium transmission case.

The litigation with Ford dragged on for four
years until in April 1952, Harry Ferguson
settled out of court for $9.25 million. As by this
time some of Ferguson's patents had expired,
Ford had to make few changes to its designs in

■ LEFT *An unusual use
to which the TE20
tractor was put was in
support of the
expedition to the South
Pole led by Sir Edmund
Hillary. The Ferguson
tractors were fitted
with special tracks and
cabs, but were otherwise
almost standard in
specification.*

order to continue building tractors with hydraulically controlled three-point hitches. The following year, Ferguson merged with Massey-Harris and Harry Ferguson turned his attention to developing a four-wheel drive system for high performance sports cars and racing cars. He died in 1960.

A particularly unusual task to which some of Ferguson's tractors were put was as vehicles for the Antarctic expedition led by Sir Edmund Hillary. The various accounts of the expedition contain numerous references to the tractors used during the course of the Commonwealth Trans-Antarctic Expedition. The tractors were used to tow sledges, unload ships and for reconnaissance in conjunction with tracked Sno-Cats and Studebaker Weasels. The Fergusons were, for at least part of the time, equipped with rubber crawler-type tracks around the (larger than standard) front and rear wheels, with an idler wheel positioned between the axles. The output of the four-cylinder engines of the Fergusons was only 28bhp, so on occasions the tractors were used linked together to increase their abilities. They were also fitted with makeshift cabs to keep the drivers warm in Antarctic conditions. The expedition members were glad of the Fergusons' abilities on numerous occasions and drove one to the South Pole itself. The tractors were commended for their simplicity, ease of maintenance and reliability, that helped them perform well in a situation never anticipated by their designer.

■ RIGHT *A Massey-Ferguson 6150 from the 1990s. Massey-Ferguson is now part of the AGCO Corporation, but the brand name still acknowledges the contribution to agriculture of the enigmatic Irishman.*

The Trend to Specialization

Much of the early experimentation in mechanizing agriculture focused on ploughing, and steam and gasoline-engined tractors were employed as an alternative to horses. It soon became apparent that a number of other implements could be pulled behind tractors or driven from their power take-offs, such as threshers, for example. After the invention of the three-point hitch, the versatility of the tractor could be exploited more fully. As a result tractors and implements became ever more specialized to suit specific farming applications. The development followed two distinct routes. One is the evolution of the specialized machine which is essentially a tractor that incorporates equipment designed to perform a specific task. Combine harvesters are examples of this. The second type of equipment is the range of increasingly specialized implements designed to be pulled behind and driven by a tractor, such as mowers, balers and seed drills.

COMBINE HARVESTERS

The combine harvester is an example of a tractor redesigned to do a single specialized job. The post-war years saw a plethora of such developments worldwide.

In its most general sense, harvesting is the picking or cutting and gathering of a crop. However, as crops are so many and various, the methods of harvesting also vary widely. Developments of the machine age have had to replace operations as diverse as the hand-cutting of wheat with a scythe and the hand-picking of fruit crops from trees. The machines referred to as "combine harvesters", or simply "combines", are so named because they combine two distinct operations in the harvesting of seed crops – namely, cutting and threshing. The combine harvester pulls the crop in with a reel over cutting blades, then compresses it and transports it to a thresher using an auger. In the thresher, the crop passes through a series of threshing rollers and sieves that separate the grain from the remainder. The grain is stored in a tank while the rest of the

■ LEFT *Prior to the development of engined harvesters, American combines were drawn by huge teams of horses such as this in Washington State.*

■ BELOW *The combine harvester became so known simply because it combined more than one harvesting operation.*

■ BOTTOM *Modern haymaking: a towed mower deposits mown hay into a trailer towed by another tractor.*

■ ABOVE *Harvesting machines, such as this John Deere 9976 designed for picking cotton, have been developed for harvesting specialized crops.*

■ FAR RIGHT TOP *The design of harvesters has progressed in recent years. This 1960s John Deere has little in the way of operator protection, while a comparable machine today would have an air conditioned cab.*

■ FAR RIGHT BOTTOM *This Claas grain combine cuts the crop and threshes it; the grain is then handled almost like a liquid as it is loaded into tractor-towed trailers that keep pace with the combine.*

plant material is discarded. Specialized combines are designed to harvest crops such as sugar cane, cotton and tobacco.

Hay, or green foliage, as it is referred to, is mowed by combine harvesters designed to cut the crop and produce tied bales. A relatively recent innovation has been the development of combines that produce large round bales

■ RIGHT *John Deere introduced the Forage Harvester in 1969 and by 1998 when this, the 480hp 6950 model was manufactured, the type had been considerably developed and refined.*

instead of smaller rectangular ones. Forage harvesters are used in making silage: they cut the crop and, by means of a spout at the rear of the harvester, deliver it into a high-sided trailer which is towed by a tractor alongside the harvester. Noted combine harvester makers currently include Case-IH, Claas, John Deere, Massey-Ferguson and New Holland Inc.

■ **HARVESTING IMPLEMENTS**
The various tasks associated with harvesting are dealt with by a vast range of towed implements. These include straw choppers that pick up and chop the debris from wheat

■ ABOVE *A specialized Fendt F220 GT machine from 1962 designed to harvest cabbages. It is powered by a 1410cc/86cu in displacement two-cylinder engine and has a six forward speed transmission.*

■ RIGHT *A diesel Fordson Major haymaking in Earl Sterndale, Derbyshire, England with an English-made rotary mower.*

■ BELOW *Specialized machinery has been developed for the harvesting of root crops, such as this machine for lifting carrots.*

harvesting and distribute it so that it can be ploughed in. For applications where combine harvesters are not used, towed implements are designed to carry out the same functions. These include rotary and disc mowers, rotary tedders and rakes which allow cut green crops to be aerated and dried. Towed balers are variously designed to make circular bales of everything from dry straw to damp silage. Round balers have now largely superseded the square balers, but both work on similar principles, requiring drive from the tractor's power take-off to gather up the cut crop and compress it into manageable bales to be transported from the field. Baler manufacturers include Bamford, Claas, John Deere, Vicon and Welger.

■ BELOW *A 1937 Fendt Dieselross F18 with a sidebar mower attachment. The noted Dieselross tractors were powered by a single cylinder 1000cc/60cu in engine.*

■ ABOVE *A 1959 Fendt FL120 tractor powered by a 1400cc/85cu in two-cylinder engine, pictured in Germany with a hay rake.*

■ BELOW *A 1998 John Deere 935 MoCo. MoCo is an acronym for mower conditioner. The 935 is intended for use with 90–150 PTO hp tractors.*

PLOUGHING

Once a crop has been harvested the land needs to be prepared for the next crop and many of the various machines used in preparing the land are of the pull-type – implements towed behind tractors. The process has to contend with widely varying ground conditions in different parts of the world. In many places with temperate climates, excessively wet soil is a problem. Not only can it be difficult for tractors to work without becoming bogged down, but excessive water impedes plant growth because no air can reach the roots in waterlogged soil. To contend with this, machines have been developed that can lay lengths of "land drain", perforated plastic piping, beneath the soil to drain the fields. A more basic method of draining fields is the excavation of ditches.

Ploughs are used to turn over the soil after harvest and the ploughed fields are then disced and harrowed to allow the seeds of next year's crop to be sown. The basic principle of the plough has remained almost unchanged since

■ ABOVE *Steam ploughing taking place at Uppingham, England during the 19th century.*

■ BELOW *Over the course of a century ploughing has become more straightforward, as the machines designed for it have become more advanced.*

■ BELOW RIGHT *Once proven, the gasoline-engined tractor soon superseded the horse as the motive power for ploughing and harrowing operations.*

a single-furrow plough was towed behind horses or oxen. It still cuts the top layer of soil and turns it over. There have been enormous changes, however, in the materials from which the plough is made, the method of propulsion, the number of furrows that can be ploughed at one time and the methods of control of the plough. John Deere's self-scouring steel plough was rightly heralded as a major innovation and ploughing was one of the primary farming tasks to which early tractors were put.

The plough has to be pulled across the entire surface of the field and numerous ways of achieving this have been tried. One notable method was the use of pairs of steam "ploughing engines" that were employed for field cultivation. They worked by drawing a plough backwards and forwards between them using a winch system rather than towing it behind a single machine. This method endured in many areas until the 1930s but, once the

■ LEFT *By the 1960s tractors such as the Fendt Farmer 2 were a common sight on European farms.*

■ RIGHT *A 1998 John Deere row crop ripper, designed for various field applications including ripping and bedding. It requires a 25–45 PTO hp tractor depending on soil type.*

■ LEFT *The tractor has become a vital farm tool even in countries which are perceived as less developed, such as this machine seen in an Albanian field.*

■ RIGHT *This diminutive English crawler is hitched to a Cooper tiller.*

gasoline tractor was completely viable, plough development concentrated on using tractors for propulsion. Ferguson's three-point linkage made the attachment of implements, including ploughs, more straightforward. The three-point linkage has now been so refined that the depth of furrows can be automatically controlled. The advent of the reversible plough allowed a tractor driver to turn all the soil in the same direction despite driving the tractor in opposite ways, to and fro across the field.

Preparation of the field requires more than ploughing and an array of other specialized implements has been devised to do this, including cultivators, harrows and stone clearers. A disc harrow is used to prepare a ploughed field for seeding while a cultivator can be used for a variety of tasks including stubble removal, mulching, aerating and turning in manure and fertilizer. Rollers can be used to make an even seed bed. Stone clearers remove stones that are turned up during ploughing and other operations; if left lying on the surface they can inhibit crop growth and damage machinery.

■ BELOW *Ploughing, tilling and harrowing can be dusty operations which is one reason that air conditioned and dust proofed tractor cabs have become the norm within farming.*

Another group of specialized implements for attaching on to tractors includes those that are designed for the distribution of manure, slurry or chemical fertilizers. They range from the "muckspreader" to the broadcaster, which spreads seed via a spinning disc, and injectors which force material into the ground.

S O W I N G ,
L O A D I N G   A N D
H A N D L I N G

The method of planting seeds depends on the type of crop being grown. Crops such as beet, lettuce, cabbage and artichokes need space to grow and therefore require planting at specific intervals. A precision seed drill is usually employed, set to plant single seeds at a specified distance apart. Seed drills for other crops can be many times wider than the tractor used for their draft. They cut numerous parallel grooves in the soil and run a supply of seed into each groove, then fill the grooves as they pass. It goes without saying that seed drills, though they still carry out the task for which Jethro Tull's machine was devised at the beginning of the 18th century, are now vastly more technically precise. The modern seed drill that enables a precise amount of seed to be sown has now generally supplanted the broadcaster type of seed distributor.

Once a crop is sown, weeds and pests have to be controlled. To do this farmers use sprayers, normally a tank mounted on the rear of the tractor, with booms to dispense the spray. Tractors adapted for this work have tall, row crop wheels that allow crop clearance and leave only narrow tracks to minimize soil compaction and crop damage. There are

numerous manufacturers of such specialized equipment around the world.

A variety of loaders have been developed, largely from the loader originally attached to the front of tractors. This purpose-built equipment includes handlers, loaders and rough terrain forklifts, all intended to speed up material and crop-handling operations for agricultural applications.

■ ABOVE *In recent years technology has been applied to the planting of seeds. John Deere developed the Max Emerge series of planters that plant several rows of seeds in one pass.*

■ LEFT *How quickly this technology has advanced is evidenced by this smaller 1958 Fendt F220 GT machine set up to do a similar job.*

■ OPPOSITE BOTTOM *A John Deere 1860 No-Till air drill is designed to open the soil, plant the seed and close the soil again in a single pass. Its tools adjust to soil types and depths with minimum work.*

■ LEFT *The John Deere 1560 No-Till drill is designed to speed up grain planting through tilling and seeding in one pass. It has a large capacity for grain and features low-maintenance till openers.*

■ RIGHT *Specialist high-clearance machines such as this self-propelled sprayer with a 24m/26ft boom are intended for use in fields of growing crops such as this oil seed rape.*

■ FAR RIGHT TOP *The sprayer booms are designed to fold in to the sides of the cab, as on this John Deere, to facilitate the sprayer's being driven on roads between fields. Note the high crop clearance.*

■ FAR RIGHT MIDDLE *This 1960 Fendt Farmer 2 FW 139 tractor is equipped with a hydraulic front loader suitable for loading hay and similar crops.*

■ FAR RIGHT BOTTOM *The JCB 520G is a loader that incorporates aspects of both the fork lift and front loader, and is suited for handling palletized products such as these rolls of turf.*

■ RIGHT *This specialized machine has sufficient clearance to pass over trees, which it sprays with a pesticide mist, as here in France.*

SPECIALIST TRACTORS

While row crop tricycle tractors were among the first specialized tractors, increasing specialization led to the production of tractors designed for particular tasks including vineyard work, cotton picking and orchard use. Such tractors have been built by numerous manufacturers, either as purpose-built models or as variants of their other models. Specialist tractors are designed for a range of tasks and some are constructed to customers' specifications. One such contemporary manufacturer is Frazier, a small British company based outside York, that is typical of many companies that produce specialized farming machinery. The company's Agribuggy is assembled from a number of proprietary components, including axles, suspension and engines, and is intended as the basis for crop-spraying and fertilizer-spreading tasks. The machines are purpose-built and offered in both diesel and petrol forms. They are designed to be adaptable and are available

■ ABOVE *One of the first specialist tractors to be developed was the tricycle-type, intended for row crop work, such as this Oliver 60.*

■ LEFT *Tractors are often used for specialist tasks such as in orchards. This Massey-Ferguson 374S is being used to collect apples.*

■ BELOW *Crop sprayers have to be suited for use in fields of part-grown crops without causing unnecessary damage to the growing plants, hence high clearance.*

■ LEFT *Sprayers are designed to be driven between rows of crops in order to minimize damage to the plants, but also require the operator to wear a mask to avoid inhaling pesticides.*

in both low ground pressure and row crop variants. Early products available in Europe included crawlers and specialist machines from the likes of Citroën-Kégresse and Latil as well as smaller vineyard tractors.

In the United States, McCormick-Deering offered specialized orchard tractors, signified by an "O" prefix. In the early 1940s the company offered the OS-4 and O-4 models, variants of the W-4 models, for orchard work. The OS-4 had its exhaust and air filter mounted underneath in order to reduce its overall height while the O-4 was fitted with streamlined bodywork which allowed the branches of fruit trees to slide over the tractor without damage. The concept of the compact tractor is now well established so that they are recognized as a bona fide agricultural product. Similar to the Agribuggy are machines from Turner, Sanderson, Schulter, Vee Pee, Westrac Triolet, Matbro, Blank and Chaviot.

■ ABOVE LEFT *These specialized Frazier machines are fitted with flotation tyres to avoid soil compaction in wet conditions.*

■ TOP RIGHT *Roadless Traction enhanced the performance of many Fordson tractors, including this 1951 Fordson E1A Major, by converting them into half-tracks.*

■ ABOVE RIGHT *The lawn tractor originated as a development of a small size tractor.*

■ RIGHT *The French-manufactured Vee Pee has low ground pressure and is used for various agricultural roles.*

■ BELOW LEFT *Tobacco is another crop that requires specialized harvesting machinery such as this example seen working in Wilson, North Carolina.*

■ BELOW RIGHT *Elineau of France manufactured this machine for spraying pesticide mist on to the small trees of apple orchards. The machine has sufficient clearance to avoid damaging the trees.*

CRAWLER TRACTORS

Paralleling the developments of the steam-powered tractor were experiments with tracked machinery known as "crawlers". The first experiments involved wheeled steam engines that were converted to run with tracks. Benjamin Holt was a pioneer of this technology, and he tested his first converted steam tractor in November 1904 in Stockton, California. Holt gasoline-powered crawlers worked on the Los Angeles Aqueduct project in 1908. Holt viewed this as something of a development exercise and learned a lot about crawler tractor construction from it, simply because dust and heat took their toll on the machines. Downtime for repairs of all makes of crawler was considerable.

World Wars I and II helped speed the development of crawler machinery in several ways. During World War I the embryonic crawler technology was soon developed as the basis of the tank, now an almost universal weapon of war. American development and use of tanks lagged behind that of Europe, partially

■ ABOVE RIGHT *The 1904 prototype steam-powered crawler tractor made by Hornsby's of Grantham, England. The company later sold its patent to American Holt in 1912.*

■ RIGHT *Early crawlers such as this one made by the Bullock Tractor Co of Chicago were chain driven; steering was by a worm drive.*

■ RIGHT *Holt and Best were among the early pioneers of crawler technology. This early machine has a disc harrow and also belt-drive pulley.*

■ BELOW *Post-war International Harvester was among the makers of crawler tractors for agricultural use, as were Caterpillar, Fiat and Fowler.*

because the United States remained uninvolved in World War I until 1917. Prior to this date the US army was still steeped in the cavalry traditions of the fighting in the Old West; by the time America became involved in the European conflict, the European nations were using tanks on the Western Front. Orders went back to the United States for tanks but in the meantime US soldiers used British and French machines, namely the Mark VI and Renault FT17 respectively. These tanks were to be produced to take advantage of America's massive industrial capacity, but they had to compete for production-line space with trucks and artillery so there was some delay. It is perhaps difficult to understand this situation

■ RIGHT *A diesel-
engined Caterpillar
crawler being used in
conjunction with an
elevator during
haymaking in England
during the late 1930s.*

■ MIDDLE RIGHT *An
early 1930s Fordson
Roadless crawler
tractor, this was the
narrow version intended
for orchards and other
confined areas.*

■ MIDDLE FAR RIGHT
*Another version of the
Fordson tractor which
has been converted
into a crawler.*

■ BOTTOM *The Bristol
tractor was manu-
factured by a small
English company that
changed hands several
times. In the late
1940s, while owned by
Saunders, the Bristol 20
used Roadless tracks
and a 16hp Austin
car engine.*

■ RIGHT *Allis-Chalmers became involved in the manufacture of crawler tractors in 1928 when it acquired the Monarch Tractor Company. The Model 35 was a 1930s model.*

when the crawler track was already well established and there had been a couple of experiments in tank development. The experimental machines included the Studebaker Supply Tank and the Ford 3-ton tank. The French tank produced in the United States was designated the M1917 and was the only US tank to arrive in Europe before the Armistice.

Tractor and crawler technology progressed as a result of these military applications. The US army had become interested in crawlers and in half-tracks – vehicles with crawler tracks at the rear and a tyred axle at the front – and in May 1931 it acquired a Citroën-Kégresse P17 half-track for assessment. US products soon followed: James Cunningham and Son produced one in December 1932; in 1933 the Rock Island Arsenal produced an improved model; Cunningham built a converted Ford

■ LEFT *International Harvester started crawler production in 1928 when it offered the TracTracTor, which then became the T-20 in 1931.*

■ BELOW *Minneapolis-Moline made this Mopower crawler loader in 1960.*

truck later in 1933; General Motors became interested and the Linn Manufacturing Company of New York produced a half-track. In 1936 Marmon-Herrington also produced a half-track, converted Ford truck for the US Ordnance Department with a driven front axle.

■ ABOVE *A 1941 Allis-Chalmers WM crawler tractor. Allis-Chalmers had adopted the orange colour scheme of Persian Orange back in 1929 just as the Depression began.*

Towards the end of the decade a half-track designated the T7 made its appearance at the Rock Island Arsenal: it was the forerunner of the Models M2 and M3 to be produced subsequently by Autocar, Diamond T, International Harvester and White.

■ ABOVE *Cletrac was an acronym for the Cleveland Tractor Company which specialized in the production of crawlers including this 9-16 Model F of 1921.*

■ RIGHT *This 1950 Fowler-Marshall VF crawler was based on the long-running and popular English Field Marshall series of tractors.*

During the 1920s Robert Gilmour Le Tourneau, an American contractor who manufactured equipment for Holt, Best and later Caterpillar tractors, developed a new system of power control that began to widen the scope of the crawler. All the control systems featured winch and cable actuation until the development of hydraulically lifted and lowered blades. One of the first British machines to be so equipped was the Vickers Vigor, developed from the Vickers VR-series crawlers. Hydraulics was just one example of the advances in technology being applied to agricultural machinery. It was first used in the late 1930s in time for bulldozers and similar machines to make a lasting impression during World War II. During the war the bulldozer earned numerous accolades and led directly to the blade-equipped tank, a type of armoured fighting vehicle still in general use.

Throughout the war years the half-track evolved and although the designs were

■ ABOVE *Converting wheeled tractors to crawlers was employed for light 4x4 vehicles such as the Land Rover. This is the Cuthbertson devised by the Scottish firm of the same name.*

■ RIGHT *The rubber tracks used on the Claas Challenger show how the idea has been refined in four decades.*

■ ABOVE *Fowler's of Grantham, England also used the name Challenger on their crawlers in the 1950s. This 35 model predates the Challenger but is of a similar design overall.*

■ LEFT *The Track Marshall crawler is manufactured by Marshall of Gainsborough, England which specialized in crawlers from 1960 onwards, the last British maker to do so.*

■ LEFT *The Roadless
RT20 crawler was
powered by a Perkins
P3 diesel engine. It was
introduced in 1954 and
intended for sales in
South America.*

standardized there are certain differences
between the models produced by the various
manufacturers. As well as the crawler
conversions to wheeled tractors made by
companies such County, Roadless and Doe,
there were even more specialized conversions
to other machines. Trackson was a crawler
track conversion offered for Fordson tractors in
the late 1920s by Trackson of Milwaukee,
Wisconsin. Later, Cuthbertson and Sons of
Biggar, Scotland converted Land Rovers to
crawler operation through the use of bogies on
a subframe assembly and sprockets driven by
the conventional axles. Recently a variation of
this idea has been offered by Toyota on one of
its luxury four-wheel-drive vehicles.

Current crawler tractor manufacturers,
beside Caterpillar and Massey-Ferguson,
include Claas, Track Marshall and
Tractoroexport. The latter is based in the
former USSR and makes the T-70 Crawler.

■ LEFT *The concept of
converting wheeled
machines to crawlers
has endured until the
present-day as this
rubber tracked Toyota
Landcruiser 4x4
illustrates.*

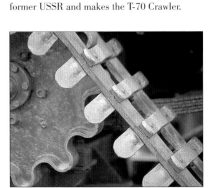

■ ABOVE *The Cuthbertson conversion for Land
Rovers relied on toothed sprockets bolted to the
driven hubs which interlock with the rubber and
steel tracks.*

■ RIGHT *A surviving Cuthbertson-converted Land
Rover from the early 1960s. Ground clearance was
increased and ground pressure decreased.*

MILITARY TRACTORS

During World War I Holt supplied crawlers to the allies while the English company Hornsby experimented with crawler tracks for tanks. The vast scale of World War II necessitated massive industrial production of all types and saw numerous tractors made that were designed for specific military purposes. The tractor types varied and included wheeled, half-track and full-track types.

In America an unusual military tractor was made by Allis-Chalmers. It was the M7 (T26E4) over-snow machine, a half-track tractor that used the entire 63bhp engine and transmission assembly from a Willys Jeep. Full-track tractors were made for the US army by International Harvester, Cletrac, Allis-Chalmers and the Iron Fireman Manufacturing Company. The International models included the TD9, TD18 and M5. The TD models were conventional full-track tractors powered by four-cylinder diesel engines, while the M5 was a high-speed tractor powered by a Continental six-cylinder engine that produced 207bhp. Cletrac manufactured the MG1 and MG2 models that were fitted with a six-cylinder

■ TOP *The Allis-Chalmers Model U was in production throughout the war years and among those exported to the UK to assist in the war effort.*

■ BELOW LEFT *The Minneapolis-Moline ZTX US military tractor of 1943 featured five gears that gave it a top speed of over 25kph/15mph.*

■ ABOVE RIGHT *During World War II tractors were used for a variety of non-agricultural tasks including work on airfields towing aeroplanes.*

■ ABOVE LEFT *As steam traction became viable the British army was quick to use Fowler engines as artillery tractors during the Boer War.*

Hercules engine that produced 137bhp. The Allis-Chalmers tractors were massive – the M4 weighed 18 tons and the M6 38 tons. Both were intended for use as artillery tractors and were powered by six-cylinder Waukesha engines.

In Britain a David Brown tractor became noted for its use by the Royal Air Force as an airfield tractor. The model was powered by an in-line four-cylinder engine of 2523cc/154cu in displacement that produced 37bhp at 2200rpm. It had a four-speed transmission and a conventional appearance.

The RAF also used a number of Roadless-converted Fordson tractors fitted with a

■ RIGHT *British Royal Engineers in the years prior to World War II landing Royal Navy equipment from a landing barge with the assistance of a Fordson tractor.*

Hesford winch for aircraft-handling duties. The Germans, Japanese and Italians made use of tractors manufactured by Latil, Somua, Hanomag, Isuzu and Pavesi. French companies Latil and Somua were captured by Germany.

There are numerous current specialist military tractors: one such specially built to meet British Ministry of Defence specifications is made by JCB. This towing and shunting tractor is designed to be manoeuvrable and

■ LEFT *The Studebaker Weasel was a light crawler machine designed by Studebaker's engineers during World War II that exerted minimal ground pressure. It was among the first of such specialist machines.*

■ LEFT *Minneapolis-Moline produced the Model NTX as an experimental military machine. It was four-wheel-drive and used standard military wheels and tyres.*

■ LEFT *A restored example of the David Brown VIG airfield tractor manufactured for the Royal Air Force and extensively used on British airfields during the conflict.*

offers tremendous traction and torque. It is ideal for moving aircraft and trailers and has a high specification cab.

Bulldozers first came to the military's attention after their use by the allies in removing beach defences, and even occupied pillboxes, in both Europe and the Pacific during World War II. Later, tanks would be equipped with bulldozer blades to assist in clearing obstacles. The Caterpillar D7 saw service in all theatres of operation during World War II and General Eisenhower credited it as being one of the machines that won the war.

As for the other US auto makers, World War II interrupted civilian vehicle manufacture, and production was turned to helping win the war. One of Studebaker's products at this time was the M29C Weasel, an amphibious cargo carrier that was a light, fully-tracked military vehicle, powered by a 65bhp six-cylinder engine, with three forward gears and a two-speed driven rear axle. It was fitted with 50cm/20in wide endless tracks and exerted a low ground pressure. This machine, designed by Studebaker's own engineers, can be regarded as one of the pioneers of the light crawler-tracked vehicle. Such machines have since become popular for specialist applications ranging from vineyard work to use on small agricultural sites where a conventional tractor or crawler would be too large.

4 X 4 TRACTORS

■ BELOW *A County Fourdrive converted Fordson tractor being used in the Solomon Islands.*

■ BOTTOM *A mid-1980s U1700L38 model of the Mercedes Unimog.*

The 1920s saw much experimentation with four-wheel-drive tractors as an alternative to crawler machines. Wizard, Topp-Stewart, Nelson and Fitch were amongst those who manufactured machines in the United States. After World War II, companies such as Roadless Traction and County Tractors offered four-wheel-drive conversions to many tractors, often using war surplus GMC truck-driven front axles. Selene was an Italian company offering 4 x 4 conversions. As the benefits of four-wheel drive came to be seen by the larger manufacturers, including the likes of Ford, John Deere and Case, they began offering their own four-wheel-drive models. This squeezed some of the small companies offering conversions. Nowadays the 4 x 4 tractor is simply seen as another conventional tractor model and four-wheel drive is often offered as an extra-cost option on machines that are also available in a two-wheel-drive configuration.

■ LEFT *On state-of-the-art tractors such as this AGCO machine-four-wheel drive is considered as just another conventional but useful feature in enhancing the tractor's performance.*

■ LEFT *A Massey-Ferguson tractor preparing a field for cultivation. Tractors have increased in size in recent years.*

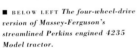

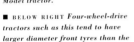

■ BELOW LEFT *The four-wheel-drive version of Massey-Ferguson's streamlined Perkins engined 4235 Model tractor.*

■ BELOW RIGHT *Four-wheel-drive tractors such as this tend to have larger diameter front tyres than the two-wheel-drive variants.*

■ ABOVE RIGHT *Some four-wheel-drive tractors such as this Fiatagri machine have different sizes of tyres at the front and rear.*

■ RIGHT *Modern tractors feature comprehensive dashboards which allow operators to monitor engine and transmission functions.*

COMPACT TRACTORS

The concept of the compact tractor can be said to have its origin in southern Europe where it was used for vineyard work. In the years immediately after World War II, NSU sold a number of its light artillery tractor, the Kettenkrad, for agricultural use, and developments also took place in the Far East. The use of compact tractors spread quickly. In England the British Motor Corporation (BMC) offered a "mini" tractor and the major tractor makers added compact tractors to their ranges.

By the mid-1980s the Japanese firm Hinomoto was making the C174 compact, which is fitted with a 1004cc/61.2cu in three-cylinder diesel engine. It produces 20hp and has nine forward gears and three reverse. The C174 is equipped with a rear-mounted power take-off and a hydraulic linkage.

Shibaura makes compact tractors for Ford and Mitsubishi makes the MT372D model as well as Cub Cadet and Case compact tractors. Iseki is another Japanese manufacturer that

■ ABOVE *The British Motor Corporation Mini tractor was aimed at the same market as the Ferguson TE20. The tractor was announced in 1965 but was shortlived and production had ceased by 1970.*

■ ABOVE *The BMC Mini was based around a 950cc/58cu in diesel version of a car engine of the time. It proved to be underpowered and was later uprated to 1500cc/90cu in.*

■ LEFT *The 1998 John Deere 5210 tractor is only 239.5cm/94.3in tall to the top of the rollbar and has an 205cm/80.7in wheelbase. Power is from a 2900cc/175cu in three-cylinder engine.*

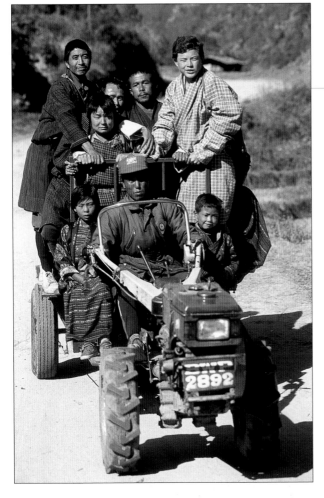

■ LEFT *The compact tractor is in use worldwide as this laden example in Bhutan shows.*

makes compact tractors for White, Bolens and Massey-Ferguson in addition to a range of larger conventional machines. In the compact category are tractors such as the TX 2140 and 2160 Models. They are powered by three-cylinder water-cooled engines, 776cc/47.35cu in and 849cc/52cu in respectively, in both two- and four-wheel-drive forms, and are suited for use with a wide range of farming implements.

Kubota is a Japanese company that was founded in the last decade of the 19th century. It began manufacturing tractors in the 1960s and claimed to be the fifth largest producer during the mid-80s. One of its products then was the compact B7100DP, a three-cylinder-powered tractor that displaced 762cc/46.5cu in and produces 16hp. It also featured four-wheel drive, independent rear brakes and a three-speed PTO.

Other compact tractor manufacturers around the world include Grillo that produces the Model 31 in Italy, Holder that makes the Cultitrac A40, and Howard that produces the Model 200 in Australia. A compact crawler, the V228, is made by Blank in Germany.

■ RIGHT *The International Harvester Cub Cadet was a diminutive tractor aimed at garden and grounds use rather than full-scale agriculture.*

■ FAR RIGHT *The BMC Mini tractor bore some resemblance to the Ferguson TE20 but struggled to compete in sales terms even with secondhand examples of the "Grey Fergy".*

THE SPORT OF TRACTOR PULLING

In the early years of the 20th century, when agriculture in the United States was booming, huge numbers of boulders had to be removed with the help of horses from massive acreages before they could be cultivated. Folklore has it that one farmer told another that he could remove a larger boulder than the other, and so almost inevitably a competition started. At the time of the outbreak of World War II, the mechanization of agriculture was well under way and by then tractors were being used for clearing boulders. Such boulder-pulling was seen as a challenge and informal competitions were introduced. The tractor that was needed on the farm all week was used for "tractor pulling" on Sundays. Over the years the tractors became bigger and the competition became ever more serious. Eventually the boulders also became a little too large to handle so the "dead-weight sled" was

■ ABOVE *Smoky Joe is a Ford 8600, based tractor puller seen here competing in an event in Warwickshire, England.*

introduced. This was a sled with weights on it, connected to the tractor by means of a chain. It was all or nothing: either the tractor took off with the sled or it lost grip and spun its driven wheels, digging itself into the track. To gain more grip, the tractors were soon loaded with anything that was heavy.

■ ABOVE *A Fiat 1000 tractor in the same event. Tractors compete in different classes depending on engine type and modifications.*

■ LEFT *One class is for modified tractors that have to retain a relatively standard appearance and bodywork. This German Deutz machine has been prepared for such a class.*

■ RIGHT *Kevin Brian's Volvo BM T800 tractor puller. Notice that the overall profile of the machine has been altered in order to accommodate the various modifications.*

Later on came the idea of making the sled heavier during the pull. A number of volunteers stood next to the track and stepped on the sled as it went past: this was, unsurprisingly, called a "step-on sled". The greater the distance covered, the higher the position. If a tractor made it to the end of the track this was called a "full pull" and the driver qualified for the finals of the day's events. Over years of pulling, the tractors continued to grow. It became harder to recruit volunteers to step on the sled because it was going faster and faster and, naturally, safety became an issue. To solve the problem, the "weight-transfer machine" was developed.

■ BELOW *A Case IH tractor puller. To increase the all-important traction, much larger than standard rear tyres are fitted where class regulations permit.*

This is a sled which has wheels at the rear end. At the start of the pull the weights are placed above the wheels. As the tractor starts to pull, the weights travel forward to the sled-plate by means of a chain. The friction increases and at some point the tractor loses traction. This principle is still in use today. The best pull is made when the tractor has a quick start. At the start of the track the sled is easy to pull, so a lot of speed can be developed. As the friction increases, the speed of the sled and tractor means that the whole unit keeps powering on and goes a few metres further.

The distance covered is now measured with infra-red equipment, and the results of a pull,

so calibrated, show that sometimes tractors come as little as 1cm/½in short of a full pull, or stop at exactly the same point. At tractor-pulling events, it is not only power that counts. Almost as important is the balance of the tractor. The sport of tractor pulling could be described as the world's most powerful motor sport, albeit not the fastest.

The tractors compete in a complex array of classes. Within the modified class come specially designed tractors, that compete in different weight classes. All types of component parts are allowed as long as the overall weight and size are within the rules. The numbers and types of engines are similarly limited by the rules. There are now also strict safety rules to protect the tractor, driver and spectators from danger. Usually, the specially constructed chassis in this class is fitted with the rear axle of a truck or excavator shovel. The internal components are replaced with stronger gears. The tyre size is limited to a diameter of 77.5–81cm/30.5–32in by the rules. The original tractor-tyre profile is always decreased

■ ABOVE *In the least restricted classes tractors are especially built with multiple engines coupled together for a massive power output.*

■ BELOW *This German Q8 sponsored machine gets its power from no less than three V12 Allison aero engines.*

by reducing the pressure in order to generate sufficient wheel-spin to prevent the tractor digging itself in while giving enough traction to move the sled forwards.

In the largest-capacity classes aircraft engines are often used today, as are gas-turbines. In the United States V8 racing-engines are very popular and in Europe tractors are fitted with up to nine engines, depending on the type and weight class.

The Super Standard or Super Stock classes feature heavily tuned standard agricultural tractors, weighing 4.5 tons. The basis of the tractor is a normal agricultural model but not much of the machine is left – everything that is normally needed for field operation is removed. The block, the clutch housing, the gearbox housing and the rear-axle have to be original although the insides of these components can be modified. To increase the engine's power, a maximum of four turbos can be fitted, as long as it all fits under the original tractor hood. The great amount of air that flows into the intake means that a lot of diesel can be injected into the cylinders. When the air is compressed by the turbos a great deal of heat is produced and

■ ABOVE LEFT *When too much is never enough: this German tractor pulling special has been constructed with four jet aircraft engines.*

■ ABOVE RIGHT *It provides spectacular tractor pulling action, but unlike some of the smaller power and weight classes, bears little resemblance to anything that can be seen in a field.*

to prevent the turbos from melting, a spray of water is injected into the intakes; this water leaves the exhaust as water vapour. To make sure this massive power reaches the wide rear tyres, numerous parts of the transmission are replaced by stronger versions, while all the unnecessary gears are removed.

Alky-burners which use methanol can be fitted: methanol burns for longer than diesel, so more power is generated and the engine suffers less stress. Numerous modifications are needed but up to 2500bhp is achievable.

The Garden Puller is the ideal start-up class. Drivers may compete from the age of eight and since this class requires little more than a

former lawnmower or garden tractor it is available to those with limited funds.

Mini-pullers are small modifieds, whose weight must include both the weight of the driver and its fuel. This class uses its own special, small sled and the tractors are custom-designed and built. They use mainly V8 engines and helicopter turbines. The power produced can be up to 3000bhp, though the average is about 1700bhp. Due to the enormous power-to-weight ratio, these machines are very hard to handle. The rear axles are mostly custom-engineered and the gearbox is little more than a single speed with a reverse gear.

■ RIGHT *The same can be said for some of the machines that rely on internal combustion engines too, and the team's name reflects the cost of this sport.*

INDEX

A

Albone and Saunderson 20–1
Allis-Chalmers 33

B

Balers 36, 73
Best, Daniel 52–3
Boulder-pulling 92
Braud 16
Bulldozers 84, 87

C

Case, Jerome Increase 44–7
Caterpillar 55, 87
Combine harvesters 70–3
Compact tractors 78–9, 90–1
Corn binders 50
Corn separators 52
Cotton gin, steam-powered 14
Cotton picking 78–9
Crawler tracks 60–3
Crawler tractors 55, 80–5
see also Caterpillar
Crop spraying 76–7
Cultivators 75

D

Dead-weight sled 92–3
Deere, John 40–3
see also John Deere
Deering Harvester Company 50–1
The Depression 34–5
Deutz 22
Diesel, Rudolph 22
Disc harrows 75
Dredging machine, steam-powered 14
Dunlop, John B. 12

E

Engines
internal combustion, early 15–16
single-cylinder 17, 20
steam 10–12, 14–17
two-cylinder 19–20

F

Fanning mill, steam-powered 16

Farm machinery, early inventions 9, 12–17
Ferguson, Harry 64–7
Forage harvesters 72
Ford, Henry 57–9
Ford, Henry II 59
Ford (company) 26, 88
Fordson see Ford, Henry
Forklifts 76
Frazier 78
Fuels 16

G

Gasoline engines, early 15–17
Goodrich, Benjamin Franklin 12–13
Goodyear, Charles 12
Grain reapers 48–9

H

Half-tracks 37, 60–3
Handlers 76
Hart-Parr 17, 18
Harvesters, combine 70–3
Hitches, Ferguson System 65
Holt, Benjamin 80, 86
see also Caterpillar
Charles Henry 54–5
Hornsby 20, 23, 86
Hydraulics 84

I

Implements
harvesting 72–3
Imported tractors 23
Internal combustion engines, early 15–6
International Harvester 18, 37
see also McCormick, Cyrus Hall

J

J. I. Case Threshing Company 16

John Deere 37, 88
see also Deere, John

K

Kégresse, Adolphe 60–3

L

Loaders 76–7

M

McCormick, Cyrus Hall 48–51
see also International Harvester
Manufacturers
competition 27–9
the Depression 34–5
early 20th century 18–23
World War II 36–7
Mass production 19–23
Massey-Harris 30, 37
Mechanization, early inventions 9–10
Meikle, Andrew 13
Military tractors 86–7
see also crawler tractors
Mowers 73

N

Nebraska tractor tests 30–1
New Holland 16

O

Orchard tractors 78–9
Otto, Nikolaus 16

P

Petter's 20
Ploughing 74–5
Ploughs, self-scouring steel 41–2
Pneumatic tyres 32–3
Production
before 1918, 19–23
the Depression 34–5
post-war boom 26–9
World War II 36–7
Pulling, tractor 92–5
Pumps, steam 10, 12

R

Rakes, rotary 73
Reapers, grain 48
Roadless Traction Ltd 88
Rollers 75

S

Seed drills 13, 76

Self-scouring ploughs 41–2
Single-cylinder engines 17, 20
Slurry spreaders 75
Sowing, loading and handling 76–7
Sport, tractor pulling 92–5
Spraying, crop 76–7
Steam power, development 10–13
Steel, for ploughs 42
Stone clearers 75
Straw choppers 72

T

Tedders, rotary 73
Three-point hitching system 65
Threshing machines 13, 16, 44–7, 53
see also combine harvesters
Tractor pulling 92–5
Tractor tests
Nebraska 30–1
Winnipeg 30
Tractors
4x4 88–9
see also Roadless Traction Ltd
compact 90–1
early mass production 18–23
first 16–17
military 86–7
specialist 78–9
Trials see tractor tests
Tricycle tractors 21, 78
Tull, Jethro 13
Two-cylinder engines 19–20
Tyres, pneumatic 32–3

V

Vineyard tractors 78–9, 87

W

Wall Street Crash 34
Waterloo Boy 17, 64
White Farm Equipment 37
Winnipeg trials 30
World War I 23, 80, 82
World War II 36–7, 84